Writing As Witness

Writing As Witness

essay and talk

Beth Brant

women's
PRESS

Some of this work has appeared in: Betsy Warland, ed., *Inversions: Writing By Dykes, Queers and Lesbians* (Vancouver: Press Gang, 1991); Linda Carty, ed., *And Still We Rise: Feminist Political Mobilizing in Contemporary Canada* (Toronto: Women's Press, 1993); Doris Seale ed., *Through Indian Eyes: The Native Experience in Books for Children* (Philadelphia: New Society Publishers, 1992); Lisa Albrecht and Rose Brewer, eds., *Bridges of Power: Women's Multicultural Alliances* (Philadelphia: New Society Publishers, 1990); *Canadian Woman Studies; Woman of Power; Akwe:kon; ColorLife; Ikon.*

CANADIAN CATALOGUING IN PUBLICATION DATA
Brant, Beth, 1941 —
   Writing as witness : essay and talk
Includes bibliographical references.
ISBN 0-88961-200-5
1. American literature — Indian authors — History and criticism. 2. American literature — Women authors — History and criticism. 3. American literature — 20th century — History and criticism. 4. Canadian literature — Indian authors — History and criticism.* 5. Canadian literature — Women authors — History and criticism — Congresses.* 6. Canadian literature — 20th century — History and criticism. 7. Indian literature — United States — History and criticism. 8. Indian literature — Canada — History and criticism. 9. Lesbians' writings, American — History and criticism. 10. Lesbians' writings, Canadian — History and criticism. I. Title
PS153.I52B73 1994   810.9'897   C94-932726-3

Editor: Mona Oikawa
Cover: Mary Anne Barkhouse   Author Photo: Amy Gottlieb
Copyright © 1994 by Beth Brant

Published by Women's Press, Suite 233, 517 College Street, Toronto, Ontario, Canada M6G 4A2.
This book was produced by the collective effort of Women's Press.
Women's Press gratefully acknowledges the financial support of the Canada Council and the Ontario Arts Council.
Printed and bound in Canada   2 3 4 5   1998

Contents

Preface

In putting together this collection of essay, talk, and theory, I hope to convey the message that words are sacred. Not because of the person transmitting them, but because words themselves come from the place of mystery that gives meaning and existence to life. To come from a people whose foremost way of communicating is through an oral tradition, I must choose each word carefully, aware of its significance, its truth, its beauty. As a writer, I must honour my ancestors, and the people I respect and love through the written way. Without writing I would be out of balance. Without the sacred I would be alone.

I have been fortunate and blessed to be invited to speak on a variety of issues. I believe this has to do with a number of things — I am an oddity to some (First Nations, lesbian, mixed-blood, urban, not educated in western "tradition"). And to some I am a friend, a writer, a talker with enough Mohawk moxie to carry it off. I am, however, not the spokesperson for the Mohawk Nation or any Nation.

I passionately believe in my people and in our continuing resistance to colonialism and the effects of the disease of racism.

I passionately believe in Native Two-Spirits who labour every day to undo the damage and heartbreak caused by homophobia within our communities and from the outside culture. I am proud to know so many and honoured that they would call me friend and sister.

This has been a difficult year for me. In April 1994, I

had a bypass operation (the second one in six years) to correct wayward and blocked femoral arteries. My recovery was slow, but good. Finishing this book was my first act of writing in over seven months. It is good to be *there* again, in that sacred place of words.

I also am honoured by these women who have especially encouraged me, nurtured me, and loved me during this painful time in my life — Mona Oikawa (who also did a loving and generous job of editing this manuscript), Nancy Chater, Connie Fife, Doris Seale, Awiakta, Ann Decter, Vickie Sears, Michelle Cliff, Celeste George, and always, Denise Dorsz. My daughters, Kim, Jennifer, Jill, and their partners, John, Alphonse, Timothy, have been there for me as well. And my beloved grandsons, Nathanael, Benjamin, Zachary, Alexander always remind me of the continuance of history, story and the People.

I also want to thank Patty Wren Smith, caretaker and wise woman of Hopscotch House in Kentucky. Her inviting me to come to the lovely and peaceful land to write is greatly appreciated. I was able to finish this book and start a new one. It is very rare for writers who are economically poor to be given opportunities like this one — a serene and lush place of spirit to engage in the acts of creation. Thank you, dear Wren.

I dedicate this book to my beloved father, Joseph Marcus Brant (1913-1991)

Don't fret.
Warriors will keep alive in the blood.

Simon Ortiz
From Sand Creek

4

The Good Red Road

Journeys of Homecoming in Native Women's Writing

There are those who think they pay me a compliment in saying that I am just like a white woman. My aim, my joy, my pride is to sing the glories of my own people. Ours is the race that taught the world that avarice veiled by any name is crime. Ours are the people of the blue air and the green woods, and ours the faith that taught men and women to live without greed and die without fear.[1]

These are the words of Emily Pauline Johnson, Mohawk writer and actor. Born of an English mother and Mohawk father, Pauline Johnson began a movement that has proved unstoppable in its momentum — the movement of First Nations women to write down our stories of history, of revolution, of sorrow, of love.

The Song My Paddle Sings

August is laughing across the sky
Laughing while paddle, canoe and I
Drift, drift
Where the hills uplift
On either side of the current swift.[2]

This is the familiar poem of Pauline Johnson, the one that schoolchildren, white schoolchildren were taught. Her love of land made her the poet she was. Yet, in reading Johnson, a non-Native might come away with the impression that she only wrote idyllic sonnets to the glory of nature, the "noble savage," or "vanishing redman" themes that were popular at the turn of the century. It is time to take another look at Pauline Johnson.

The Cattle Thief

How have you paid us for our game? how paid us for our land?

By a *book*, to save our souls from the sins *you* brought in your other hand.

Go back with your new religion, we never have understood

Your robbing an Indian's *body*, and mocking his *soul* with food.

Go back with your new religion, and find — if find you can —

The *honest* man you have ever made from out of a *starving* man.

You say your cattle are not ours, your meat is not our meat;

When *you* pay for the land you live in, *we'll* pay for the meat we eat.[3]

It is also time to recognize Johnson for the revolutionary she was. Publicized as the "Mohawk Princess" on her many tours as a recitalist, she despised the misconceptions non-Natives had about her people. Her anger and the courage to express that anger also made her the poet she was. She was determined to destroy stereotypes that categorized and diminished her people. Breaking out of the Victorian strictures of her day, she drew a map for all women to follow. She had political integrity and spiritual honesty, the true hallmarks of a revolutionary.

The key to understanding Native women's poetry and prose is that we love, unashamedly, our own. Pauline Johnson wrote down that love. Her short stories are filled with Native women who have dignity, pride, anger, strength, and spiritual empowerment.[4]

Pauline Johnson was a Nationalist. Canada may attempt to claim her as theirs, but Johnson belonged to only one Nation, the Mohawk Nation. She wrote at great length in her poems, stories and articles about this kind of Nationalism. She had a great love for Canada, the Canada of oceans, mountains, pine trees, lakes, animals and birds, not the Canada of politicians and racism that attempted to regulate her people's lives.

In 1892, she was writing articles on cultural appropriation, especially critiquing the portrayal of Native women in the fiction of the day. She tore apart popular white writers such as Charles Mair and Helen Hunt Jackson for their depictions of Native women as subservient, foolish-in-love, suicidal "squaws." Her anger is tempered with humour as she castigates these authors for their unimaginative use of language and for their insistence on naming the Native heroines "Winona" or a derivative thereof.[5]

Pauline Johnson is a spiritual grandmother to those of us who are women writers of the First Nations. She has been ignored and dismissed by present-day critics and feminists, but this is just another chapter in the long novel of dismissal of Native women's writing.

Pauline Johnson's physical body died in 1913, but her spirit still communicates to us who are Native women writers. She walked the writing path clearing the brush for us to follow. And the road gets wider and clearer each time a Native woman picks up her pen and puts her mark on paper.

I look on Native women's writing as a gift, a give-away of the truest meaning. Our spirit, our sweat, our tears, our laughter, our love, our anger, our bodies are distilled into words that we bead together to make power. Not power *over* anything. Power. Power that speaks to hearts as well as to minds.

Land. Spirit. History, present, future. These are expressed in sensual language. We labour with the English language, so unlike our own. The result of that labour has produced a new kind of writing. I sometimes think that one of the reasons our work is not reviewed or incorporated into literature courses, (besides the obvious racism) is that we go against what has been considered "literature." Our work is considered "too political" and we do not stay in our place — the place that white North America deems acceptable. It is no coincidence that most Native women's work that gets published is done so by the small presses: feminist, leftist or alternative. These presses are moving outside the mainstream and dominant prescriptions of what constitutes good writing. The key word here is "moving." There is a movement going on that is challenging formerly-held beliefs of writing and *who* does that writing. And it is no coincidence that when our work is taught, it is being done so by Women's Studies instructors and/or those teachers who are movers and hold beliefs that challenge those of the dominant culture. This is not to say that *all* women's studies are as forward-thinking as we would like. At Women's Studies conferences, the topics of discussion usually center on white, European precepts of theory and literature. I am tired of

8

hearing Virginia Woolf and Emily Dickinson held up as the matriarchs of feminist and/or women's literature. Woolf was a racist, Dickinson was a woman of privilege who never left her house, nor had to deal with issues beyond which white dress to wear on a given day. Race and class have yet to be addressed; or if they are discussed, it is on *their* terms, not *ours*.

We are told by the mainstream presses that our work doesn't sell. To quote Chief Sealth — "Who can sell the sky or the wind? Who can sell the land or the Creator?" The few women of colour who have broken through this racist system are held up as *the* spokespeople for our races. It is implied that these women are the only ones *good* enough to "make it." These women are marketed as exotic oddities. (After all, we all know that women of colour can't write or read, eh?)

Pauline Johnson faced this racism constantly. The "Mohawk Princess" was considered an anomaly, and I can't say that things have changed all that much. I think of Pauline a lot, especially when I rise to read my stories. For like her, "My aim, my joy, my pride is to sing the glories of my own people."

Because of our long history of oral tradition, and our short history of literacy (in the European time frame) the amount of books and written material by Native people is relatively small. Yet, to us, these are precious treasures carefully nurtured by our communities. And the number of Native women who are writing and publishing is growing. Like all growing things, there is a need and desire to ensure the flowering of this growth. You see, these fruits feed our communities. These flowers give us survival tools. I would say that Native women's writing is the Good Medicine that can heal us as a human people.

9

When we hold up the mirror to our lives, we are also reflecting what has been done to us by the culture that lives outside that mirror. It is possible for all of us to learn the way to healing and self-love.

It is so obvious to me that Native women's writing is a generous sharing of our history and our dreams for the future. That generosity is a collective experience. And perhaps this is the major difference between Aboriginal writing and that of European-based "literature." We do not write as individuals communing with a muse. We write as members of an ancient, cultural consciousness. Our "muse" is *us*. Our "muse" is our ancestors. Our "muse" is our children, our grandchildren, our partners, our lovers. Our "muse" is Earth and the stories She holds in the rocks, the trees, the birds, the fish, the animals, the waters. Our words come from the very place of all life, the spirits who swirl around us, teaching us, cajoling us, chastising us, loving us.

The first known novel written by a Native woman was *Cogewea — The Half-Blood.*[6] Written by Hum-Ishu-Ma, Okanagan Nation, in 1927, this novel depicts the difficulties of being called half-breed. Hum-Ishu-Ma concentrates on the relationship the female protagonist has with her Indian grandmother, and how Cogewea does not turn her back on her people, although she is courted and temporarily seduced by the white world. Hum-Ishu-Ma worked as a migrant labourer, carrying her typewriter everywhere with her, snatching moments to write. Again, I am reminded of Pauline Johnson and her Indian women who remain steadfast in their Aboriginal beliefs and spiritual connections to their land and people and the desire to make this truth known.

Fifty years later, Maria Campbell wrote her ground-breaking *Half-Breed*,[7] taking up the theme of despair that comes as a result of the imbalance that racism and poverty create in a people. Maria has a grandmother whose words and strength give her nurturance and hope and a way back to the Good Red Road. The Good Red Road is a way of life among Native peoples that is one of balance and continuity. Again, this seems to be the overwhelming message that Native women bring to writing. Creating a balance in their protagonists' worlds, remembering what the Elders taught, recovering from the effects of colonialism. This is not to say that Native women's writing contains "happy" endings or resolutions. In fact, to wrap things up in a tidy package is not following the Good Red Road — it's a falsehood. Perhaps this is what irritates white critics — our work is said to have no plots! If we won't conform, how can these conformist reviewers write reviews?! Perhaps the questions should be: why are critics so unimaginative in *their* writing? Why are they so ignorant of what is being written by my sisters? Why is a white-European standard still being held up as the criteria for all writing? Why is racism still so rampant in the arts?

Leslie Marmon Silko published her novel, *Ceremony*,[8] in 1976. In 1992, *Almanac of the Dead*,[9] by the same author, was published. Between those years and after, Paula Gunn Allen, Louise Erdrich, Jeannette Armstrong, Anna Lee Walters, Ella Deloria, Beatrice Culleton, Ruby Slipperjack, Cyndy Baskin, Betty Bell, Lee Maracle, Velma Wallis and Linda Hogan also published novels.[10]

In the field of autobiographical works, the number of Native women's books is outstanding. Minnie Freeman, Maria Campbell, Ruby Slipperjack, Alice French, Ignatia Broker, Lee Maracle, Madeline Katt, Florence Davidson, Mary John, Gertrude Bonnin, Verna Johnson and others[11] tell their stories for all to hear, and we become witness to the truth of Native lives. Throughout these writings, strong female images and personas are evident. The Cheyenne saying, "A Nation is not conquered until its women's hearts are on the ground," becomes a prophecy about Native women's writing. First Nations women's hearts are not on the ground. We soar with the birds and our writing soars with us because it contains the essence of our hearts.

Deep connections with our female Elders and ancestors is another truth that we witness. Grandmothers, mothers, aunties, all abound in our writing. This respect for a female wisdom is manifested in our lives; therefore, in our writing.

Poetry seems to be the choice of telling for many Native women. In our capable hands, poetry is torn from the elitist enclave of intellectuals and white, male posturing, and returned to the lyrical singing of the drum, the turtle rattle, the continuation of the Good Red Road and the balance of Earth. We write poems of pain and power, of ancient beliefs, of sexual love, of broken treaties, of despoiled beauty. We write with our human souls and voices. We write songs that honour those who came before us and those in our present lives, and those who will carry on the work of our Nations. We write songs that honour the every-day, we write songs to food; we even incorporate recipes into our work. Chrystos, Mary TallMountain, Nora Danhauer, Mary Moran,[12] are just a few who have written about the joys of fry bread, salmon, corn soup and whale blubber, then turn around and give instruction for preparing these treats! To me, this is so ineffably Indian. Mouths salivating with the descriptions of our basic foods, readers are then generously offered the gift of how to do this ourselves. No wonder the critics have so much trouble with us! How could food possibly be art?! How can art remain for the elite if these Native women are going to be writing recipes in poems? What will the world come to, when food is glorified in the same way as Titian glorified red hair?

There are numerous books of poetry written by Native women.[13] Our poems are being published in forward-thinking journals and magazines, although there are still the literary journals that wish to ghettoize our work into "special" issues, which, if you will notice, happen about every ten years or so. And their editors are usually white and educated in the mainstream constructs of European sensibility.

When I was asked in 1983 to edit a Native women's issue of the feminist journal, *Sinister Wisdom*, I did not expect the earthquake that *A Gathering of Spirit* would cause. Eventually, this work became a book, published in 1984, then re-issued by Firebrand Books and by Women's Press in 1989.[14] Perhaps there is a lesson here. When Natives have the opportunities to do *our own* editing and writing, a remarkable thing can happen. This thing is called *telling the truth for ourselves* — a novel idea to be sure and one that is essential to the nurturance of new voices in our communities. I conduct writing workshops with Native women throughout North America, and the overriding desire present in these workshops is to heal. Not just the individual, but the broken circles occurring in our Nations. So, writing does become the Good Medicine that is necessary to our continuation into wholeness. And when we are whole our voices sail into the lake of *all* human experience. The ripple-effect is inevitable, vast and transcendent.

There are women who are writing bilingually. Salli Benedict, Lenore Keeshig-Tobias, Rita Joe, Beatrice Medicine, Anna Lee Walters, Luci Tapahonso, Mary TallMountain, Nia Francisco, Ofelia Zepeda, Donna Goodleaf[15] are just some of the Native women who are choosing to use their own Nation's languages when English won't suffice or convey the integrity of the meaning. I find this an exciting movement within our movement. And an exciting consequence would be the development of *our own* critics, and publishing houses that do bilingual work. Our languages are rich, full of metaphor, nuance, and life. Our languages are not dead or conquered — like women's hearts, they are soaring and spreading the culture to our youth and our unborn.

Pauline Johnson must be smiling. She was fluent in Mohawk, but unable to publish those poems that contained her language. There is a story that on one of her tours, she attempted to do a reading in Mohawk. She was booed off the stage. Keeping her dignity, she reminded members of the audience that she had to learn *their* language, wouldn't it be polite to hear hers? Needless to say, impoliteness won the day.

From Pauline Johnson to Margaret Sam-Cromarty,[16] Native women write about the land, the land, the land. This land that brought us into existence, this land that houses the bones of our ancestors, this land that was stolen, this land that withers without our love and care. This land that calls us in our dreams and visions, this land that bleeds and cries, this land that runs through our bodies.

From Pauline Johnson to Marie Baker, Native women write with humour. Even in our grief, we find laughter. Laughter at our human failings, laughter with our Trick-

14

sters, laughter at the stereotypes presented about us. In her play, *Princess Pocahontas and the Blue Spots*,[17] Monique Mojica, Kuna/Rappahannock, lays bare the lies perpetrated against Native women. And she does it with laughter *and* anger — a potent combination in the hands of a Native woman. Marie Baker, Anishanabe, has written a play that takes place on the set of an Indian soap opera, "As the Bannock Burns." Baker's characters are few — the Native star of the soap, and the new co-star, a Native woman who gives shaman lessons to wannabes. In the course of the one-act play, the star shows the would-be shaman the error of her ways under the watchful eyes and chorus of a group of women of colour. Not only does Baker poke fun at the Greek chorus concept in theatre, she turns this European device to her own and *our* own amusement in a caustic but loving way, to bring the would-be shaman to a solid understanding of herself and her own tradition.

Sarah Winnemucca, Suzette La Flesch,[18] and Pauline Johnson also left them laughing as they took their work on the road. To tell a good story, one has to be a good actor. I remember my grandad telling me stories when I was little, punctuating the sentences with movement and grand gestures, changing his facial expressions and voice. I think we are likely to witness more Native women writing for the theatre. Margo Kane has ventured into that place with her play *Moon Lodge*. Vera Manuel has written *The Spirit in the Circle*, addressing the painful past of residential schools and the painful present of alcoholism and family dysfunction. But she also posits a vision for the future out of these violent truths. Spider Woman's Theatre has been writing, producing and acting in their plays for a number of years. And Muriel Miguel, one of

15

the Spiders, has done a one-woman show incorporating lesbian humour, Native tricksters and female history. Native women are writing the scripts for their videos and directing and producing these films. How Pauline Johnson would have loved video!

As Native women writers, we have formed our own circles of support. At least once a week, I receive poems and stories in the mail, sent to me by First Nations women I know and some I have never met. It thrills me to read the words brought forth by my sisters. This is another form our writing takes — being responsible and supportive to our sisters who are struggling to begin the journey of writing truth. The WordCraft Circle, a mentoring program that matches up more experienced writers with our younger brothers and sisters, was born out of a Native writers' gathering held in 1992 in Oklahoma. I am currently working with a young, Native lesbian, and it moves my heart that it is now possible for lesbian Natives to give voice to *all* of who we are. Keeping ourselves secret, separating parts of ourselves in order to get heard and/or published has been detrimental to our communities and to our younger sisters and brothers who long for gay and lesbian role models. I am proud of the burgeoning Native lesbian writing that is expanding the idea of what constitutes Native women's writing.

There are my sisters who have internalized the homophobia so rampant in the dominant culture and that has found its way into our own territories and homes. These sisters are afraid and I understand that fear. Yet, I ask for a greater courage to overcome the fear. The courage to be who we are for the sake of our young and to honour those who have come before us. Courage of the kind that Connie Fife, Chrystos, Barbara Cameron, Sharon Day,

Susan Beaver, Nicole Tanguay, Two Feathers, Donna Goodleaf, Janice Gould, Vickie Sears, Donna Marchand, Mary Moran, Elaine Hall, Lena ManyArrows, Shirley Brozzo and many others have displayed.[19] Writing with our *whole* selves is an act that can re-vision our world. The use of erotic imaging in Native lesbian work becomes a tool by which we heal ourselves. This tool is powerfully and deftly evident in the hands of these writers, especially the poems of Janice Gould and Chrystos. In my own work, I have explored such themes as self-lovemaking, and the act of love between two women[20] as a way to mend the broken circles of my own life, and hopefully to give sustenance to other women who are searching for new maps for their lives. But Native lesbian writing is not only about sex and/or sexuality. There is a broader cultural definition of sexuality that is at work here. Strong bonds to Earth and Her inhabitants serve as a pivotal edge to our most sensual writing. Like our heterosexual sisters, Native lesbians who write are swift to call out the oppressions that are at work in our lives. Homophobia is the eldest son of racism; they work in concert with each other, whether externally or internally. Native lesbian writing *names* those twin evils that would cause destruction to us.

A major theme in the work of Vickie Sears, Cherokee Nation, is the power over children's bodies by the State.[21] Sexual abuse, physical abuse, emotional abuse are "normal" occurrences to the girl-children in Vickie's short stories. Herself a survivor of the foster-care system, Sears finds her solace and empowerment through the things of Earth and the love between women. Her short stories emphasize these possibilities of self-recovery. Indeed, one could say that much of Native lesbian writing celebrates

17

Earth as woman, as lover, as companion. Woman, lover, companion celebrated as Earth. Two-Spirit writers are merging the selves that colonialism splits apart.

Recovery writing is another component in the movement of Native women writers. Recovery from substance abuse, as well as racism, sexism and homophobia. Two Feathers, Cayuga Nation, is a wonderful example of this kind of recovery writing, as is Sharon Day of the Ojibway Nation.[22] Again, Chrystos, Menominee poet, excels in the naming of what it feels like to be hooked and in thrall to the substances that deaden the pain of being Native in the 20th century. Highly charged with anger, this recovery-writing is, at the same time, gentle with the knowing of how difficult the path is toward the Good Red Road. There is empathy and compassion in the telling of our people's struggle to stay clean and sober, there is rage against the State that employed *and* employs addiction to attempt our cultural annihilation. Many of my short stories focus on that moment between staying sober and taking "just one" drink. The characters are caught in that timescape of traditional Native "seeing," and the unnatural landscape of colonization through addiction. In my stories, as in my life, Creator brings gifts of the natural to "speak" to these characters. It then becomes a choice to live on the Good Red Road, or to die the death of being out of balance — a kind of "virtual reality," as opposed to the real, the natural.

Pauline Johnson knew firsthand the effects of these attempts at annihilation. Her father, a Chief of the Mohawk Nation, was a political activist against the rum-runners who would have weakened his people. Severely beaten many times by these smugglers and murderers, his life was considerably shortened. Many of Pauline's stories

18

are filled with righteous anger against the whiteman who wished to rape our land, using alcohol as a weapon to confuse and subjugate us. I think she would applaud the recovery-writing and name it for what it is — an Indian war cry against the assassination of our culture.

Oral tradition requires a telling and a listening that is intense, and intentional. Giving, receiving, giving — it makes a complete circle of Indigenous truth. First Nations writing utilizes the power and gift of story, like oral tradition, to convey history, lessons, culture and spirit. And perhaps the overwhelming instinct in our spirit is to love. I would say that Native writing gives the gift of love. And love is a word that is abused and made empty by the dominant culture. In fact, the letters l-o-v-e have become just that, blank cyphers used frivolously to cover up deep places of the spirit.

I began writing when I turned forty. I imagine the spirits knew I wasn't ready to receive that gift until I was mature enough and open enough to understand the natural meaning of love. I believe that the writing being created by First Nations women is writing done with a community consciousness. Individuality is a concept and philosophy that has little meaning for us. Even while being torn from our spiritual places of home, having our ancestors names stolen and used to sell sports teams, automobiles, or articles of clothing; having our languages beaten out of us through residential school systems even while having our spirits defiled and blasphemed, our families torn apart by institutionalized violence and geno-cide; even after this long war, we still remain connected to our own.

Our connections take many forms. I, as a Mohawk, feel deep spiritual bonds towards many who do not come from my Nation. These people, Carrier, Menominee, Cree, Cherokee, Lakota, Inuit, Abenaki and many others, are like the threads of a weaving. This Mohawk and the people of many Nations are warp and woof to each other. While the colour and beauty of each thread is unique and important, together they make a communal material of strength and durability. Such is our writing, because such is our belief-system. Writing is an act that can take place in physical isolation, but the memory of history, of culture, of land, of Nation, is always present — like another being. That is how we create. Writing with all our senses, and with the ones that have not been named or colonized, we create.

Janice Gould, Maidu Nation, has written, "I would like to believe there are vast reserves of silences that can never be *forced* to speak, that remain sacred and safe from violation."[23] I feel that these sacred silences are the places *from* which we write. That place that has not been touched or stained by imperialism and hatred. That sacred place. That place.

Like Pauline Johnson, mixed-blood writers find those sacred places in the blood that courses through our bodies, whispering, "come home, come home." Although we have never left that home, in a sense we have been pulled and pushed into accepting the lies told about our Indian selves. For those of us who do not conform to a stereotype of what Native people "look like," claiming our identities as Native people becomes an exercise in racism: "Gee, you don't look like an Indian." "Gee, I didn't know Indians had blue eyes." "My great-great-grandmother was a Cherokee princess, does that make me an Indian too?" After a while it almost becomes humourous, even as it's tiresome. Perhaps the feeling is

20

that we're getting away with something, that we are tapping into unknown strengths, for which we are not entitled. And how the dominant culture loves to quantify suffering and pain! And how well it has worked to divide us from each other and from our self. Colourism is another face of racism. And we write about that, exposing our fears of abandonment by the people we love, the people whose opinion matters, the very people who, in our dreams, whisper, "Come home, come home." Yet, mixed-blood writing is also what I have been examining; for most of us are bloods of many mixes and Nations. Linda Hogan, Chickasaw Nation calls us "New People." New People are the survivors of five hundred years of colonial rule. Our grandmothers' bodies were appropriated by the conquerors, but the New People have not forgotten that grandmother, nor the legacy she carried in her womb.

In Mexico, a story is told of La Llarona. It is told that she wanders throughout the land, looking for her lost children. Her voice is the wind. She weeps and moans and calls to the children of her blood. She is the Indian, the mother of our blood, the grandmother of our hearts. She calls to us. "Come home, come home," she whispers, she cries, she calls to us. She comes into that sacred place we hold inviolate. She is birthing us in that sacred place. "Come home, come home," the voice of the umbilical, the whisper of the placenta. "Come home, come home." We listen. And we write.

Notes

1. E. Pauline Johnson as quoted in Betty Keller, *Pauline: A Biography of Pauline Johnson* (Vancouver: Douglas & McIntyre, 1981): 5.
2. E. Pauline Johnson, "The Song My Paddle Sings" in *Flint & Feather* (Toronto: Hodder & Stoughton, 1931).
3. E. Pauline Johnson, "The Cattle Thief" in *Flint & Feather*.
4. E. Pauline Johnson, *The Moccasin Maker* (Tucson: University of Arizona, 1987).
5. E. Pauline Johnson, "A Strong Race Opinion on the Indian Girl in Modern Fiction," originally published in the *Toronto Sunday Globe*, 22 May 1892.
6. Hum-Ishu-Ma (Mourning Dove), *Cogewea, The Half-Blood* (Lincoln: University of Nebraska, 1981).

   Hum-Ishu-Ma's mentor was a white man. My reading of *Cogewea* is that much of it was influenced by his perceptions, not Hum-Ishu-Ma's.
7. Maria Campbell, *Half-Breed* (Toronto: McClelland & Stewart, 1973).
8. Leslie Marmon Silko, *Ceremony* (New York: Viking Press, 1977).
9. Leslie Marmon Silko, *Almanac of the Dead* (New York, Toronto: Simon & Schuster, 1991).
10. Paula Gunn Allen, *The Woman Who Owned the Shadows* (San Francisco: Spinsters/Aunt Lute, 1983); Louise Erdrich, *Love Medicine* (Toronto, New York: Bantam, 1989); Jeanette Armstrong, *Slash* (Penticton: Theytus, 1986); Anna Lee Walters, *Ghost-Singer* (Flagstaff: Northland, 1988); Beatrice Culleton, *In Search of April Raintree* (Winnipeg: Pemmican, 1983); Ella Deloria, *Water Lily* (Lincoln: University of Nebraska, 1988); Ruby Slipperjack, *Honour the Sun* (Winnipeg: Pemmican, 1987); Ruby Slipperjack, *Silent Words* (Saskatoon: Fifth House, 1992); Cyndy Baskin, *The Invitation* (Toronto: Sister Vision, 1993); Linda Hogan, *Mean Spirit* (New York: Atheneum, 1990); Lee Maracle, *Ravensong* (Vancouver: Press Gang, 1993); Velma Wallis, *Two Old Women* (New York: Harper Perennial, 1993); Betty Louise Bell, *Faces In the Moon* (Norman: University of Oklahoma Press, 1994).
11. Minnie Freeman, *Life Among the Qallunaat* (Edmonton: Hurtig, 1978); Ignatia Broker, *Night Flying Woman: An Ogibway Narrative* (St. Paul: Minnesota Historical Society, 1983); Lee Maracle, *Bobbie Lee: Indian Rebel* (1976; reprint, Toronto: Women's Press, 1990); Verna Patronella Johnston, *I Am*

22

Nokomis, Too (Don Mills: General Publishing Ltd., 1977); Madeline Katt Theriault, *Moose to Moccasins* (Toronto: Natural Heritage/Natural History Inc., 1992); Janet Campbell Hale, *Bloodlines* (New York: Harper Perennial, 1993); Wilma Mankiller, *Mankiller: A Chief and Her People* (New York: St. Martin's Press, 1993); Bonita Wa Wa Calachaw Nunez, *Spirit Woman* (New York: Harper & Row, 1980); Helen Pease Wolf, *Reaching Both Ways* (Laramie: Jelm Mountain Publications, 1989); Zitkala-Sa, *American Indian Stories* (Washington: Hayworth, 1921); Ida Patterson, *Montana Memories* (Pablo: Salish Kootenai Community College, 1981); Alice French, *My Name is Masak* (Winnipeg: Pequis, 1976), and *Restless Nomad* (Winnipeg: Pemmican, 1991).

12. Chrystos, "I Am Not Your Princess," *Not Vanishing* (Vancouver: Press Gang, 1988); Mary TallMountain, "Good Grease," in *The Light On the Tent: A Bridging* (Los Angeles: University of California, 1990); Nora Marks Dauenhaur, "How to Make a Good Baked Salmon," *The Droning Shaman* (Haines: Black Currant, 1985); Mary Moran, *Métisse Patchwork*, unpublished manuscript.

13. Poets include Beth Cuthand, Joy Harjo, Marie Baker (Annharte), Janice Gould, Wendy Rose, Diane Glancy, Awiakta, Elizabeth Woody, Joanne Arnott, Carol Lee Sanchez, Paula Gunn Allen.

14. Beth Brant, ed, *A Gathering of Spirit* (Sinister Wisdom Books, 1984; Ithaca: Firebrand, 1988; Toronto: Women's Press, 1989).

15. Lenore Keeshig-Tobias, *Bird Talk* (Toronto: Sister Vision, 1992); Rita Joe, *Poems of Rita Joe* (Halifax: Abenaki, 1978); Beatrice (Bea) Medicine, "Ina," *A Gathering of Spirit*; Anna Lee Walters, *Talking Indian: Reflections on Survival and Writing* (Ithaca: Firebrand, 1992); Nia Francisco, *Blue Horses For Navajo Women* (Greenfield Center: Greenfield Review, 1988); Ofelia Zepeda, unpublished manuscript; Donna Goodleaf, unpublished manuscript.

16. Margaret Sam-Cromarty, *James Bay Memoirs* (Lakefield: Waapoone Publishing, 1992).

17. Monique Mojica, *Princess Pocahontas and the Blue Spots* (Toronto: Women's Press, 1991).

18. Sarah Winnemucca and Suzette La Flesch (Bright Eyes) travelled and performed in the United States, talking about their people in poetry and story, within the same time frame as Pauline Johnson's career.

23

19. Makeda Silvera, ed., *Piece of My Heart* (Toronto: Sister Vision, 1991); Will Roscoe, ed., *Living the Spirit: A Gay American Anthology* (New York: St. Martin's, 1988); Connie Fife, ed., *The Colour of Resistance* (Toronto: Sister Vision, 1993); Gloria Anzaldua, ed., *This Bridge Called My Back* (Albany: Kitchen Table Press, 1981) are just four of the collections containing Native lesbian work. See also Connie Fife, *Beneath the Naked Sun* (Toronto: Sister Vision, 1992); Chrystos, *Not Vanishing, Dream On, In Her I Am* (Vancouver: Press Gang, 1988, 1991, 1993); Janice Gould, *Beneath My Heart* (Ithaca: Firebrand, 1990).

20. Beth Brant, *Mohawk Trail* (Ithaca: Firebrand, 1985; Toronto: Women's Press, 1990); Beth Brant, *Food & Spirits* (Vancouver: Press Gang, 1991).

21. Vickie Sears, *Simple Songs* (Ithaca: Firebrand, 1990).

22. Sharon Day and Two Feathers, unpublished manuscripts.

23. Janice Gould, "Disobedience In Language: Texts by Lesbian Natives" (Speech to the Modern Language Association, New York, 1990).

Anodynes and Amulets

We are surrounded by magazines, journals and idiom of the New Age religion. This religion has no specific dogma or doctrine other than heavy reliance on paraphernalia and language, some of it "borrowed" from Indigenous cultures. In one magazine, a shamanic tour is offered, for which a person may spend several thousands of dollars to travel to holy places of spirit with an "experienced" shaman. Supposedly the end result will be communication with whatever spirits choose to present themselves to the pilgrims. Aside from the obvious distress to land that will be travelled upon, trampled upon, there is the arrogance and blasphemy implied by the belief that spirits will come at the bidding of pilgrims who have money to buy them. I realize this is a basic tenet of christianity, especially the Catholic church, but it seems that those folks who are anxious to have an experience with *other-worldly* beings are the same people who would declare they are colour-blind or refer to Indigenous peoples of any continent as "our Natives." There is the same kind of patronizing and ethnocentric behaviour being acted out as that of the missionary and the liberal.

In another journal, an interview with a "channeller" is displayed. A channeller is a person who is taken over by the spirit of another and who speaks with the other's voice. Channellers come in both sexes — a bleached

25

blonde woman in Chicago channels a South Asian man, named Ramtha, who lived many centuries ago. A pale, bland man is channelling the voice of the archangel Michael. All channellers are white. I am reminded of a letter Linda Hogan received from a white woman who claimed she channelled the spirit of a dolphin, and therefore also laid claim to being a "sister" to Linda. Linda was bemused by both claims. She guessed the channeller assumed that Indians did this activity all the time and would welcome a non-Indian into the ranks of our Nations. But as Linda said to me, "What self-respecting Dolphin would speak *to* her [the woman who wrote the letter], much less *through* her?" We laughed together over this latest attempt to colonize our belief systems, but under the laughter was anger. It's not enough that they appropriate *us*, they also want to subsume the spirit of all living things.

In these magazines are advertisements for computer astral charts, books on metaphysical subjects and shamans, books on Hindu and Buddhist masters, books chronicling the spirit-chasers' adventures on aboriginal lands. There are books about white people taken aboard alien ships, then returning to earth at the astonishment and confusion of their families and neighbours, ultimately acquiring agents to hawk their stories to publishers and movie producers. There are advertisements for weekends of spiritual harmony with whomever is a popular practitioner at the time. Even has-been actors, hoping to shore up their waning bank accounts and visibility, have become groupies or shills for these practitioners. I assume their jobs are to lend some show biz glamour to a dull act!

There are all-women and all-men retreats. The women

26

are supposed to get in touch with the goddess within. The men are supposed to get in touch with their fathers and their maleness. Of course, male or female, drumming and dancing are required, feathers are worn, "names" are given, lots of hugging and getting in touch with feelings. O Capitalism, how mighty art thou! For thousands of dollars, thee will give something to fill the aching hearts and souls of a bereft society.

There are crystals everywhere. Advertised in new-age magazines, in feminist journals, in catalogues. The mining of these stones has caused a depletion and collapse of old caves and caverns, especially in parts of South America. I guess it has not occurred to consumers and salesmen that the reason there *are* special places that resonate are because the stones were *there*, not hanging around the necks of gullible and weary pilgrims who quest for some anodyne to a cold and loveless society.

I cannot document when this movement started to gain force. In reading the many newspapers and magazines, one might come to the conclusion that the new-age religion is a natural phenomenon that had to come into being as a resistance to materialism and conspicuous consumption of goods and services. It would seem that people had lost ties to a spiritual base. But I am talking about white people, because in all the information I have gathered, this religion and/or movement is populated by Anglos and most especially, Anglos with money to spend. This is not a "free" or inexpensive religion. If you want it bad enough, you have to pay. How can a spiritual base be bought? How can a spirit be called with money? But there it is — you pay your money, you get *it*. The new-age is merely the old-age — capitalism cloaked in mystic terminology, dressed in robes and skins of ancient and

Indigenous beliefs. This is all so familiar to me. The Blackrobes with their cross and rum proclaimed a new age for Indigenous peoples. The Spanish, the French, the British, the Dutch proclaimed a new world for themselves. And while the colonialists appropriated land and bodies, the new-age appropriates belief and turns it to their own use. This religion is the colonizing of spirit *and* spirits.

If the new-age religion is a resistance to materialism, where is the resistance? If it is a movement, where is it moving to? Nowhere do I see the formation of a catalyst that challenges the existence of the status quo. What I do see are bits and pieces of this and that to improve individual life. What kind of movement is it that only encompasses an individual lifestyle? Where is community in this religion/movement?

In all the propaganda of the new-age I've read, there is no mention of lesbians or gay men. This is not surprising in itself; the surprise comes when I see so many gay men and lesbians following this religion. I am especially disheartened by the new-age making inroads into the lives of people who are HIV positive or have AIDS. While I fully believe that people have choices and the desire to be comforted in times of sorrow and travail is universal, a popular belief amongst new-agers is that we have chosen our destinies and illnesses. In other words, my friends "chose" to get AIDS and die painfully and horribly. This sounds like fundamental christianity to me. If we were all straight and white, in other words, "good," we wouldn't have nearly the trouble we are having. And if we've "chosen" to be of colour, we better soon discover our place, catering to the whims of the white population that wants what they think we have — a mysterious communication with spirits that the whiteman can't see or hear.

If I didn't know how insidious racism can be and how it is wrapped in the arms and legs of the institutions of state, church and media, I would feel great compassion for the pilgrims of the new religion. To be honest, I do feel a pity for them. Is no one happy? Is no one at peace? And yet, my pity does not render me incapable of challenging the emptiness of the dominant culture's belief system. There *is* no belief, except in that of money and power over. This belief has spilled into my communities. There are Native "plastic shamans" who do sweats, who give workshops, who sell tapes to hungry white souls in need: feminists, christians, PWAs, all the hungry white souls. And I find this as unforgivable and blasphemous as I do a Lynn Andrews who writes lies and sells those lies.

The new-age religion is so ethereal. Ethereality is light and wispy. Earth and Her creatures are not. A tree is sturdy, sheds leaves, turns colour, exhibits cycles of regeneration. A stone is quiet, finds its way into water or earth. A bull moose moves through forest, munching on green things, growing antlers, rutting in a noisy, community ritual. These are the physical evidences of spirituality in my belief system. So is sexual activity, laughing, making soup, taking a bath, having a menstrual cycle, taking my grandchildren to see turtles. Perhaps it is the solidity of Native beliefs that are so attractive to white people who grew up on a diet of christian miracles. But belief in Earth and Her magic is just not "mystical" or "ethereal" enough for people who seem to need a more colourful and packaged product in which to invest.

Leslie Silko, when asked by a white woman how to

learn more about Indian religions, replied, "Get involved in environmental issues. Help save Earth from destruction. This is our religion." However, I think Leslie knew, as I do, that her reply was not what the white woman wanted to hear. She wanted to hear of ceremony, of ritual, of gods and goddesses, of secret societies, of secrets. And those who want to invest in our spirituality do not want to hear that we would sometimes like to have their presence when we are trying to protect our land and culture; that sometimes it would be useful to hear their voices raised in protest when our land and culture are being threatened. The ethos of the new-age is passivity and dilettantism.

I am distressed at attempts of the women's movement to appropriate symbols and history of other cultures and renaming that "women's culture" or "lesbian culture." One can only come from one's own culture and class. We are not born full-blown into feminists or lesbians. We come from families, from communities, from religions, from Nations that inform us as human beings. It may be possible to discard or put away those values that reek of racism, sexism, and homophobia, but we can't remake ourselves into an image that is just another take on a racist formula. I am incensed when white feminists want to insist that Native religions have goddess figures. That is a European concept and has no place in our beliefs. The same holds true of wicce or witchcraft. Mohawk Got'go' is *not* to be defined by European models. It is difficult to exorcise the predominance of the English language, but it is possible to understand that although we may share a common language, *my* definition is not necessarily one that is parallel to that of a Euro-christian culture.

Arrogance that exhibits itself through language,

through ethnocentrism is a hallmark of the new-age. The belief that human beings are more important than any other part of Creation. The belief that holy places and holy beings are defined by capitalism. I once wrote a poem, years ago, about many old women gathered together to perform a ceremony. The "ceremony" was a celebration of the ordinary — a bird's feather, a cradleboard, a beaver skin. I was amazed that many white people asked me if this was a "real" ceremony, a genuine Mohawk ritual. Amazed, because they misunderstood the whole essence behind the words. No, this was not a "real" ceremony; I wouldn't describe or write about a religious event that takes place in my community. But this poem was my attempt at sharing what is holy to me, the magic of things that are common and useful. That the commonness of a bird's feather is precisely what makes it magic. That mystery is fused with the everyday. That Beaver once wore this skin and her spirit lives in the warm fur. That when a Turtle rattle is shaken, that *is* the voice of Turtle. That laughter accompanies spiritual celebrations. That old women touch and value each other. I was struck by the sad inability of some to see the elemental, physical, sensuous foundation of my belief. They would rather have been privy to some "exotic" ritual than to accept a gift from me. They saw a pretty package, but were unaware of what it contained, because it was impossible for them to believe that a bird's feather is as valuable as the human holding it.

To the new-ager, a superficial feeding of the bare spots of the heart is what is seen as important. I call this racism because underneath the questing is really the belief that they are superior and only need to partake of certain magics to uphold the fallacy that they are dispensing largesse to the great unwashed and uncultured. In other words, the new-age is doing Indigenous peoples a *favour* by stealing our ceremony and ritual. Does this sound familiar? Isn't this what the christian churches have done for centuries and continue to do?

The similarities between christianity and new-age religion are exhibited in the certainty that *their* way is *the* way. Collecting monies and souls, dispensing amulets and anodynes (for a price), and telling the non-believers that the path to fulfilment is paved with money — the seeker's money, that is. I think a channeller would be perfectly comfortable in Vatican City. And the Pope would feel at home in the luxurious surroundings of Ramtha's house.

Now, I may be giving the impression that I am an intolerant, hateful woman. I am not. I *am* an angry woman. And a sad woman. What on Earth can heal all those broken people who sincerely look for alternative ways to find wholeness? I don't know, but I will suggest activism. I will suggest political involvement in issues that threaten land and peoples. I realize this holds no glamour or reward. But I am also much more concerned with what can heal the broken Nations of my people.

I remember a concert I attended years and years ago. Chris Williamson (a white feminist singer) was performing. She was talking about Leonard Peltier and his incarceration for a crime he didn't commit. Her speech was going along fine until she made the statement that "everyone" should get to know a Native American. "It will make your life richer." As if we were placed on Earth to enrich white people's lives! As if we stood around on corners, hoping to be picked up by white people so they can have an "experience." We *have* enriched white people's lives. Natives and people of colour have worked someone else's farms, have raised white babies, have coddled and cajoled white men, have made life easier for white women by providing domestic work, have cooked food for white stomachs while going hungry ourselves, have fought in their armies in their seemingly never-ending wars. Yes, we have made their lives richer, and continue to do so as they appropriate our spirituality. None of this was given. It was taken. And I find this fascination with and practice of Indigenous religions a rape.

First Nations people are seen as a stereotype. There is no thought to the fact that we work, we play, we worry, we make love. There is no thought that our Elders like gossip or Bingo. There is no thought that we rush off to catch planes, write poetry, wash clothes, walk picket lines, put cars together. The new-age does not see us in our human spectrum. It is easier and less complicated for them to view us as artifacts or symbols that are waiting to be scooped up, inspected, *used* as they see fit.

There is no doubt that we see the universe through a different set of values and beliefs. It is impossible for non-Natives to *feel* the sorts of emotions that are called upon when Indigenous peoples speak about ancestors, about Earth, about the symbiosis that exists between human and animal. Non-Natives come from another psychic and physical place. *We* have been here for centuries. Our ritual has meaning because we are *from here*, not because we plucked it out of the air and thought it would be fun or nice to perform. It is in us, perhaps even in the DNA of our cells, to give ourselves over to what whispers to us from the corn, from Deer, from Heron, from the rock that resides on the bottom of the waters. We have a relationship with the beings who share Earth with us.

I believe that non-Natives can love the wild spaces, can feel the excitement of Cranes lifting off into sky, can testify to the beauty that still lives abundantly in North America. I believe this, for I have heard it expressed and written about. I also know that *our* love comes from a commitment to Earth; She is our Mother, She holds the bones of our ancestors in trust. The very trees hold our stories. Our spirits hover and gather around us. We know the words to use to bring them closer, to intervene for us.

I long for a conclusion to the new-age religion, and in its place, a healthy respect for sovereignty and the culture that makes Nationhood. We do not object to non-Natives praying *with* us (if invited). We object to the theft of our prayers that have no psychic meaning to them. Our belief systems contain the cosmos of history and regeneration, of harmonious and balanced thought that has travelled on this land, touching Aboriginal mind, intertwining with beings who live alongside us. This cannot be bought with capitalistic or colonial greed. It is ours. We have always been generous peoples, giving food and knowledge to those who visited us. But what is in our blood is neither for sale nor for a fast spiritual fix. If non-Natives are hungry, let them learn to make food from what is in *their* blood.

Keep the Drum Playing[*]

Se:khon. It is true that Doris Seale and I have met for the first time at this gathering, but we have been close friends for over ten years. My non-Native friends seem to have a hard time grasping this concept — that people can be intimate without ever having held hands or looked into each other's eyes. Friendships can be made through letters, through phone calls, and *especially* through the exchange of poems, stories, ideas and politics.

This panel has been brought together to discuss the future of Native art and the people who create that art. What kinds of things we will expect to see, to hear, to feel, to touch, to imagine. When I asked Joe Bruchac what I should talk about, he said, "Anything you want." And since I am a Mohawk woman, you *know* I will talk about whatever I want!

I think that all of us in this room are here because of the warriors who walked the path and fought the battles that have made our lives, our choices less painful and maybe a little easier to bring to flower. Writing is never easy, but our relatives such as Pauline Johnson, D'arcy McNickle, Scott Momaday, Leslie Silko, Simon Ortiz, Carol Lee Sanchez, and many others, have brought us the hope

---

* From a speech given at the first Native Writers' Gathering, Oklahoma, 1992.

of possibility, the knowledge that *story* is who we are, and why we are here.

In our long and complicated history with the European invaders, our story was stolen and made over into a tale that was palatable to them, the thieves who wished to eradicate all memory of us, who wished to eradicate *our* memory. I believe that memory is like the drum, one tap and the sound resonates and reverberates into our very soul. One poem, one story, one painting, and our hearts and bodies respond to the message — we are here. We remember.

My father was my teacher. He was a scholar, though his name will never be on an institution's plaque or on a book cover. He knew so much about our history — not just Mohawk history — and he gave and gave this knowledge to all who wanted to learn. He especially wanted to give to Natives. He felt that we had lost so much, had been robbed of so much. Daddy believed that an educated Indian was a strong Indian — educated in *our* history, *our* way, *our* story. Although Daddy worked hard to go to university (he worked on the line making cars in the day, then went to school at night), he never felt that formal western education was the only way to learn. There was not an elitist bone in his body. (Although he had his share of Mohawk arrogance.) He believed in books. If it had the words Indian or Native on the cover, he bought it or borrowed it from the library. He taught himself, he taught his children, he taught Natives who took his adult education courses on Indian history and culture. When I began to write, he was thrilled, not because I had books published, but because the tradition of telling truth would continue. Last year, when I told Daddy this gathering was going to happen, he smiled his sweet smile and said, "Oh, I would like to go to that. It sounds good." My father passed on to the Spirit World last December, but he is here, and it is good.

The tradition of telling truth. This is a long and honourable one in our culture, and in our words. When E. Pauline Johnson wrote, "My aim, my joy, my pride is to sing the glories of my own people," she was honouring our tradition of truth-telling and story. Writing at the turn of the century and the early 1900s, this Mohawk woman had seen ugly change brought to her people. Educated by her white mother in literature and the Classics, she brought a new kind of writing into the world: fictionalized accounts of the horrors and dangers of colonialism, stories of strong and proud Native women. We owe much to Pauline, she was a harbinger to all of us here. It saddens me that so many Native children are not learning her stories and poems. While some may think her language is old-fashioned and dated, her politic remains clear, fresh and beautiful. She is our Grandmother. What we do today as writers must honour her.

Our writers of today are marking new directions on the path that was originally mapped out for us. We are making new signposts. There is a strong movement of Native gay and lesbian poetry and prose. We write honestly about homophobia from our own communities, as well as those outside us. We write about love, about sex, about the history of Two-Spirits. There are more voices coming from the working-class and working poor amongst us. Many of us are teachers, continuing the tradition of passing on our history and language. We write about that. We write about being mothers, fathers, maids, teachers, factory workers, healers; we write about being writers, artists. *We write about being human.* We write about our relationship with Earth and Her creatures. All of this is political, but when has our writing *not* been that way?

So many of us write. Few of us get published, not because the work isn't good, but because the publishers and presses are not there to commit to us. We all know that Tony Hillerman will be published, while our own writers are neglected. It seems that the whiteman's version of who we are is still more credible than what we have to say for ourselves. We all would like to see more First Nations publishers, more presses, more money to enable this work. Sometimes I think we should set up a Lotto club and buy lottery tickets in our various communities and put the winnings into a fund for publishing books!

We need to talk more about forming our own ways of getting our work to the many Aboriginal peoples who are waiting to hear what we say. For all of us speak to our people and for our people. I think Native teachers and educators need to use our books, our words, in their classrooms, and not just the ones published by major (white) presses. We desperately need our own agents, our own reviewers, our own magazines. How many times have we been misunderstood, and therefore not paid attention to, because of a white editor's or reviewer's blissful ignorance? I remember sending a short story to a fancy magazine and being rejected because the editor didn't know why I named a cat in the story, The Prophet. He seemed to think that I was being "precious," because the cat was a being who was bringing visions to a young man. If he had had the humility to ask, I would have told him of Tecumseh and The Prophet, those great Shawnee warriors and brothers who fought until the day they died for their people's freedom. He also stated that the older

Native woman in the story would not have been accepting of her son's homosexuality! How would he know? But this kind of imperialism festers in the white publishing world.

I also feel that white publishers (as a rule) do not want to open themselves to the stories that are not full of pathos and victimization. They don't want to take a chance on our humanness. This would mean they'd have to give up their historical amnesia when it comes to us and our way. They like to see us as "plight" rather than the dedicated survivors we are.

There is also a flowering of feminist writing coming from our Native sisters. Some of us may have been uncomfortable with the word, but not the force behind the word. While the (white) media may like to think that the feminist movement is Gloria Steinam and Susan Faludi, we know different. And I think it's time we realize that feminism is not just about white women, it is about all of us. Writers like Lee Maracle, Betty Bell, Kate Shanley, argue for a feminism that encompasses sovereignty, children, Earth, class, race, sexuality, and all the varied and exciting aspects that make community possible. We are changing the face of feminism. It is no longer a middle-class, white movement for acknowledgement and better pay — it is about uranium in our drinking water, fetal alcohol syndrome, family violence, a life for the generations to come. We are writing about this in passionate and poetic language. We are not afraid to bring "family secrets" into the open air of this new day. The "secrets" belong to all of us.

It is no surprise that most First Nations writers are also activists. Organizing, gathering, mentoring, demonstrating, picketing. Our writing is, and always has been, an attempt to beat back colonization and the stereotyping of our Nations. But the writing is *not* a reaction to colonialism, it is an active and new way to tell the stories we have always told. Native writing is only about one hundred years old. Previously, we told the lessons, told the history, told the ancestors' biographies. At this time, we write, but we also tell. I can't think of any Native writer who does not like to read his or her work aloud. This is what makes the writing harmonious and circular. We write, we speak, we write. It all belongs together, for our oral ways are not lost or forgotten. Some of us write longhand, some use typewriters, some use computers; none of *this* is important, because the idea of story has not changed.

I think the future of First Nations writing is where we are living today. I see more writers being born, more vision being created. As long as we live, we will tell our story.

I would also like to say, on this beautiful Oklahoma morning, that when I found out I was to speak with Simon Ortiz, I was thrilled beyond words. Reading his story-poem "Change In A Good Way," allowed me to know for the first time, that it was possible to write about the things that were so familiar to me — working-class Indian people interacting with their white neighbours, making small changes in the imperialist's doctrine of the history between Red and white. This is the way my family had talked, had worked, had lived. When I heard Simon read that same story the other night, I wept. My own life as a writer had come full circle. I want to thank Simon for that story and for the beauty of his writing. I want to thank all the relatives who came before us and the ones who gather at this moment in our history. The story that made possibility and future for me, was reminding me, once again, that we only have to tell what is honourable and truthful — the story of our lives.

Nia:wen.

Recovery and
Transformation[*]

Last weekend in Minneapolis was the first gathering of
gay and lesbian Two-Spirits — The Basket and the Bow.[1]
This gathering was a joyful one, a reunion of sorts —
much like a pow wow, where we go to see old friends,
share stories with family, catch up on tribal happenings,
take care of Indigenous business — the difference being
that this reunion was largely between people who had
never met.

Cree, Ojibway, Mohawk, Athabascan, Paiute, Lakota,
Metis; so many Nations represented by our Queer citizens.
Our initial shyness soon was dispelled by our great
happiness in being with each other. *Us*, our family.

We talked, we laughed, we wept together. We told our
stories, we listened, we touched. And as I talked with my
sisters and brothers and listened, listened to the voices
telling their lives, two words kept insisting their message
onto my brain.

Recovery. Transformation.

Recovery. Transformation.

Recovery is the act of taking control over the forces

*   Speech given at the National Women's Studies Conference,
Minneapolis, Minnesota, 1988.

that would destroy us. Recovery from alcohol and drug use — most definitely. But another kind of recovery is taking place in our family. Recovery from the disease of homophobia. This disease has devastated my Indian family as surely as smallpox, alcohol, glue-sniffing and tuberculosis have devastated our Nations. Recovery is not an act that ignores the disease. Recovery is becoming *stronger* than the disease. The evidence was there before my eyes. For two days we assured each other that we won't self-destruct any more, we won't be shamed any more, *we won't go away.*

We come from an ancient tradition. Our languages, sabotaged by outsiders for almost five hundred years, *still* contain words for us.[2] The exorcisms that the christian church has conducted over us have not worked. Yet, we are in mourning for all those who came before us and are to follow, those who did not and do not *know* that we are many, and that we have formed battalions to fight this disease. We ask the questions: How many of our teen-age brothers and sisters commit suicide because they think they are alone in their gayness? Can these suicides only be defined as despair over living in poverty and a lost culture? Who will dare to ask these questions if not *us?*

Transformation. The act of changing the function or condition of. We begin by changing the internalization of homophobia into a journey of healing. There is a coming-clean that takes place on this journey. We cleanse ourselves according to our spiritual beliefs and world-views. Albert told a story of when he felt ready to participate in the Sun Dance, but was fearful of homophobic reaction. He went to a Medicine Woman who told him, "You will present yourself to Creator, not the peo-

44

ple." Albert took this message to his heart. A Sun Dance can last hours or days, until a communion with Creator is made. Albert made this communion and presented himself with a full knowledge of who he is and what he is to his community. I like that phrase, *present yourself.* It seems to fit us so much better than *coming out.*

On our separate, yet communal journeys, we have learned that a hegemonic gay and lesbian movement cannot encompass our complicated history — history that involves so much loss. Nor can a hegemonic gay and lesbian movement give us tools to heal our broken Nations. But our strength as a family not only gives tools, it helps *make* tools.

Presenting ourselves to Creator means realigning ourselves within our communities and within our spiritual selves to create balance. Balance will keep us whole. To be a First Nations Two-Spirit means to be on a path that won't be blocked by anyone or anything. To be an Indian lesbian or gay man at this time means that a woman like me won't have to search and re-search for the Barbara Camerons to keep me sane and unafraid.[3] The Barbara Camerons of the future are here in the printed word, on the tapes, on film, on this stage, in this audience. There will be no cover-up in this recovery — by white imperialism or by my own people. There are too many of us now. We are too savvy, too knowledgeable of the colonialist's mind, too well-versed in our politics to allow ourselves to be hidden again under the layers of anthropological bullshit, or through denial, or the looks of anger that come from our heterosexual brothers' and sisters' eyes.

If our existence can be denied, then so can the existence of infant mortality or the chipping away of our lands, stone by stone. If you believe in the existence of wild rice, blue herons, the moon — you have to believe in us. For we are part of all that exists.

Recovery means that we transform ourselves. Presenting ourselves means that we transform our world. This has been made so clear. Many of us are substance-abuse counsellors, lawyers skilled in sovereignty issues. We are health care workers, teachers, midwives, artists, actors, writers, mothers, fathers, lovers. Our political acts — and our very survival *is* a political act — are transforming the face of Indian Country and marking roads into the heart of North America.

There is a personal recovery taking place in me. For the last two years I have been on a journey of physical illness, culminating in a small stroke and a ten hour surgery to bypass a congenital condition in my femoral artery that had almost stopped the flow of blood to my legs. This journey took many turnings I would not have chosen for myself, such as the incredible pain when I walked even a few feet. And this pain also clouded my emotional being, my spiritual being. I began to distrust people who loved me. I was unkind to those who would have helped me. And I was unkindest to myself and gave up the thing that I loved — writing. I welcomed my oldest "friend" — self-hatred.

As the stroke was beginning in my arm, travelling to my right leg, then moving up to my face, I shouted "NO!" The echoes of that *no* bounced around in my ears. Terrified and almost incapable of thought or action, the words *not yet, not yet, not yet*, were sounding like a drum with each heart's beat. Later in the hospital I thought about the arrogance of those words, *not yet.* I, who had forgotten the joy of life, had the fear of losing it.

46

When I came home after the long days of healing, I wanted to celebrate the rejuvenation of my body and spirit by making love. Denise was fearful of hurting me, but I persisted, feeling that sex was another kind of beginning for me, because this too was something I had denied myself. My participation in such a primal ritual was an important component in my wellness.

I have thought about the transformative power of sexuality. The *magic* of sex that has been trivialized by a dominant and empty society. *Our* sexuality is despised because sex is despised, unless shrouded in misogynist and/or racist winding sheets. That sad, dominant society that embraces death even as it fears it, does not understand that recovery is transformation, and transformation is an act of love. But we have always known that acts of love are the very reason we are here.

Lesbian and gay Natives will become and are becoming the Elders of our people, giving counsel and wisdom. We are presenting ourselves in the fullest way possible for us. This can only be a good thing for our communities. Because we do not search for ourselves alone, as individuals. It is a community effort. I have always thought that Native people bring a particular kind of beauty to this world. Lesbian and gay Natives expand that beauty by bringing our transformative love to those who would receive it — our people.

Nia:wen.

Notes

1. The Basket and Bow gathering took place June 18-19, 1988 in Minneapolis, Minnesota. The title of the gathering comes from an Ojibwa story that tells of an Elder giving a child the choice of which path to follow. Some girlchildren selected the basket. Some boychildren selected the bow. And some girls and boys chose both, claiming the two-spirited path as the one they would follow. This story was related to me by Sharon Day.

2. Nadle, shopan, a-go-kwa, ayekkewe, bade, winkte, geenumu gesallagee, ma ai, pote are words in Navajo, Aleut, Chippewa, Cree, Crow, Lakota, MicMac, Shoshone respectively, that are still in use. See also, Maurice Kenny, "Tinselled Bucks;" Will Rosco, ed., *Living the Spirit* (New York: St. Martin's Press, 1988); and Walter Williams, *The Spirit in the Flesh* (Boston: Beacon Press, 1986).

3. Barbara Cameron is the co-founder of Gay American Indians. Founded in the early seventies, GAI has been a resource for all Native Two-Spirits who think they are alone. The organization is based in San Francisco. Barbara Cameron has been an inspiration to all Native lesbians. Writer, activist, mother, freedom fighter, she worked for all of us, and gave us courage to keep going.

From the Inside
Looking at You*

The title of this workshop, "From the Outside Looking In," implies that those of us on this panel are somehow on the outside of the normal, the real and the truth. I must protest this abrogation of our thoughts and words to fit a white-defined framework of what constitutes racism and writing. As a Mohawk, I am very much inside my own world-view, my own Nation, and I am looking at you — the descendants of the European fathers who colonized that world.

My people are an oral people. This means that our stories, our history, our value-systems, our spirituality have been given to us by the spoken, not the written word. And because our words were spoken, it is important that we choose words carefully, and that we *listen* with equal care. I want you to know this because as a Native woman who writes, as well as speaks, I feel a great responsibility to share words that are truthful. I have heard non-Natives say that truth is a "relative thing." We

---

*   From a panel entitled "From the Outside Looking In: Racism and Writing," given at the Gay Games Literary Festival: Crossing Borders, Vancouver, B.C., 1990.

49

do not believe in that philosophy. Indeed, that philosophy has been a force behind the onslaught of colonialism.

During the physical and cultural genocide perpetrated upon my people, the Europeans came with a book, and that book was called the holy bible. Through the use and enforcement of that book, those written words, everything that *we* had known was shattered. Our world was splintered, and we are left with the excruciating task of finding the pieces of our world and making it right again, making it balanced again. For this is at the heart of our search — restoring balance within our communities in a dominant culture that has gone amok with greed and worship of individualism. What does this have to do with racism and writing? Everything.

Literacy is a new concept to us, the Indigenous peoples of North America. As of today, 50 percent of my people are either illiterate or functionally literate (by western standards). We do not have the seeming luxury of research. We cannot go to a book and find out who was gay or lesbian, who said this at what time, who said that at what time — for books, like the bible, are distortions of the truth — starting with the Jesuits and continuing with modern-day "priests" like Grey Owl, Lynn Andrews and Tony Hillerman. We must rely on memory, our Elders, our collective dreams to find those pieces that were cut from us. The written word, the bible book almost destroyed our faith in who we are, and so, we have come to view the written word with suspicion and apprehension. The lies about us in the form of letters, sentences, paragraphs proliferate like a virus and spread negation and invisibility. "Indian experts" are inevitably white men and women who presume to do the talking for us as if we are a dead people.[1] But, you get the picture: poor, dead Indians, with no one to speak on our behalf except for the liberal whiteman. When it comes to "folk-tales" or "myths," they scour the continent for "genuine" Natives. But it also seems that we have had the last laugh in the circus of anthro-gladiators. Our Elders have told us that many so-called informants deliberately gave wrong information to the anthros. An Indian joke, folks!

Those of us who are Native and have *chosen* to write are a fast-growing community. This has not been an easy path to travel. For myself, this entails being in a constant state of translation. Those of you for whom English is a second language will understand some of what I say. Not only am I translating from the spoken to the written, but also writing in a language that is not my own. When I sit in front of my typewriter, there are times I literally cannot find the words that will describe what I want to say. And that is because the words I want, the words I "hear," are Mohawk words. But you see, my Mohawk language was virtually destroyed in my family. My grandmother and grandfather were taught, in residential school, that Mohawk was a bad thing. To speak Mohawk, to be Mohawk. After hundreds of years of emotional and physical assault on us for using the language Creator gave us, we now find it in our best interests to communicate with the language the enemy forced on us. Therefore, I bend and shape this unlovely language in a way that will make truth. Because the language of the enemy was a weapon used to perpetuate racism and hate, I want to forge it in a new way, as a weapon of love. I also feel that a piece of writing is not finished until it is spoken. I read my work aloud as I write, after I write and often when I am sleeping. My stories are *meant* to be spoken. My work is *meant* to be said out loud. In sign or by voice, storytelling is a natural act. I also feel that I must say this — I do not write for you who are white. I write for my own. Another natural act.

This leads me to ask you who are white to listen to us, the Aboriginal peoples whose land you occupy. What you will hear from us is the truth of how it is with us. The truth does not lie in the realm of colonial supremacy, nor in the kingdom of imperialistic propaganda. No one can speak for us but us. There may be those of European descent who want to be our allies in the elimination of racism. I welcome you. My people welcome you. Dionne Brand has said that if a white writer introduces a character of colour into their writings, that writer must be account-able for his or her place in that writing.[2] Why do you write about a person of colour? This is an important question, but the answer is even more so, since *our* history of the last five hundred years is so entangled with yours. I do not say that only Native peoples can write about Natives. I will never say that. I do say that you can't steal my story and call it your own. You can't steal my spirit and call it yours. This has been the North American Dream — stolen land, stolen children, stolen lives, stolen dreams — and now we are *all* living the nightmare of this thievery. If your history is one of cultural dominance, you must be aware of and *own* that history before you can write about me and mine. This can be liberating for you. I'm sure there are many in this audience who are recovering from alcohol, drug and food addictions. Ra-cism is also an addiction, one from which it is possible to recover. There are no Twelve-Step programs for this one, however. This recovery is a solitary one, even with support.

Those of us who are Native have internalized the racism that devastated our lands like biological warfare. For some, this is reason enough why we don't or can't write. For centuries we have heard the words used to describe us: dumb Indian, lazy Indian, ugly Indian, drunken Indian, crazy Indian. It has been nearly impossible to not have these messages encoded on our brains. Messages that play back in our heads whenever we step outside "our place." Messages that still proliferate from the media, from the institutions, from the christian church. To write or not to write is a painful struggle for us. Everything we write can be used against us. *Everything we write will be used against us.* And I'm not talking about bad reviews. I'm talking about the flak we receive from our own communities as well as the smug liberalism from the white, "literary" enclave.

Writing is an act of courage for most. For *us*, it is an act that requires opening up our wounded communities, our families, to eyes and ears that do not love us. Is this madness? In a way it is — the madness of a Louis Riel, a Maria Campbell, a Pauline Johnson, a Crazy Horse — a revolutionary madness. A love that is greater than fear. A love that is as tender as it is fierce. Writing is also a gift. For me, it is a precious gift given to me in my fortieth year of life on Earth. Along with the gift came instruction to use this gift on behalf of love.

I feel a personal responsibility and a strong desire to tell the truth. Sometimes that desire is a physical craving as I sit in front of my machine, sweating, hurting, struggling with a *contra* language to conceive new words. I desire to make rage a living testament. I desire to heal. I desire to make beauty out of circumstances that are not beautiful. I desire truth.

53

I also want to share this desire. I want allies and lovers in this war against racism. I want honesty from allies and lovers. I want acts of love to be committed in all our languages.

It is said that the Mohawk language was first spoken by a woman, and it became her responsibility to teach all who came from her womb. Racism and homophobia were unknown words to her and her descendants. I have also heard and dreamed that her first words were those of thanks — thanks for the paradise that was entrusted to her care and respect — a trust that has been handed down story after story after story. The carriers of the bible book brought a new kind of story to us, a story that resounds with cacophony and cruelty. We are holding on to what is still intact — our spirit, our strength. And when I use the enemy's language to hold onto my strength as a Mohawk lesbian writer, I use it as my own instrument of power in this long, long battle against racism.

Nai:wen.

Notes

1. A notable exception is Richard Drinnon's, *Facing West: The Metaphysics of Indian Hating and Empire Building* (Minneapolis, MN: University of Minnesota Press, 1980), an excellent analysis of racism from the "wild west" to the jungles of Vietnam. This book has been sadly neglected in favour of more palatable books on the "plight" of the Indian.
2. Yet another panel on "Racism and Writing." This one took place at West Words, a writing workshop for women held every year in Vancouver, B.C. Dionne spoke eloquently to the subject.

Physical Prayers

I was told a story.[1] On feast days, after the food was
eaten, after the dancing, after the singing prayers, another
kind of prayer was begun. Men and women chose who
they wished to be partnered with, retired to places on
open ground, and commenced the ritual of love-making.
As the touching, stroking and special play was being
enacted, and the sighs and cries were filling the air, the
spirit of each individual became a communal prayer of
thanksgiving. Sexuality, and the magic ability of our
bodies to produce orgasm was another way to please
Creator and ensure all was well and in balance in our
world.

As a creative human being who is also Native and
Two-Spirit, I will not make distinctions between sexuality
and spirituality. To separate them would mean to place
these two words in competition with each other, to rate
them in acquiesence to white-European thought, to deny
the power of sex/spirit in my life, my work.

In white North America, sex and spiritual beliefs are
commodities, packaged and sold in the markets of free
enterprise. From the golden halls of Vatican City to the
strychnine-laced paths of Jonestown, the story is the
same: confine the minds and bodies of the followers,
especially the minds and bodies of those who are poor
and of colour, and make sure the women answer to only

one person — a white male who can rape at will, who can dole out forgiveness and redemption for a price, who decides which life is expendable and which is not. The emperors of free enterprise claim belief in god and family. Yet, I believe at the root of their belief-system is a hatred of sex. A people who despise sex must also despise their god. Why else do they make a vast chasm between the two? Does their attempt to make both god and sex into images that fit a white-male thesis (christianity) mean that they will like themselves more?

As a lesbian, I know that the dominant culture only sees me as a sexually uninhibited creature. As a Native lesbian, I know the dominant culture does not see me at all, or sees an abberation of a "dead" culture. By daring to love and have sex with another like myself, I have stepped beyond any boundary the emperors could have imagined. In the emperors' eyes, sexual freedom means freedom from *them*, a scary thought to be sure. There is no money to be made from the likes of me, except from the porn trade, and even then, lesbian lovemaking is just a prelude to the "real" thing — penetration by a man.

I became a lesbian in my thirty-third year of life. I had crushes on girls as a youth, and even had a sexual encounter at the age of sixteen with an older woman of eighteen who asked if she could eat my cherry. Of course I said yes! Curiosity, desire, longing to break any rules, I let my cherry be eaten and look back on that moment with a sweet nostalgia. I don't know if I was born a lesbian, and I don't care. I find the recent preoccupation with nature vs. nurture very tiresome and dangerous. In my thirty-third year of life I was a feminist, an activist and largely occupied with discovering all things female. And one of those lovely discoveries was that I could love women sexually, emotionally, and spiritually — and all at once. This is why I choose to be lesbian. It makes me more complete in myself, and a whole woman is of much better use to my communities than a split one. Now, in my fifty-third year of life I am a feminist, an activist and a grandmother and still in the early stages of discovery and wisdom. But I do think of that distant moment when an older woman of eighteen gave me such pleasure and allowed me to know my body's desires. I am not one who wonders, "What if?" yet I am fairly certain that if I had followed my inclination, I may have become that older woman's "lady," and perhaps would have slipped easily into the gay life of the 50s. I was/am very much a child of my class — I would have gotten a job cashiering or as a saleslady; my lover would have worked on the line, and we would have made a home in a fairly traditional butch/femme way; I probably never would have become a writer, much less a woman who says the word lesbian out loud in front of strangers! And my being Native, being Mohawk, might have been a source of distant amusement or puzzlement to my lover. We would have been women of our time and class. I expect my family would have reacted in much the same way they did years later — accepting a white woman into the family because I loved her. But our lives would have been hidden from the dominant culture.

The blending of Native and lesbian, which to me, has been a sensual and pleasing journey, is not so pleasant to some of my own Native sisters and brothers of the heterosexual persuasion. I could discount their anger, and/or off-handedly blame colonialism (which *is* to blame), but I desire to look further into the heart of this anger and imagine a revelation that could possibly transform us as individuals and community members. This is something I cannot do alone.

I don't know if all First Nations had words or expressions to connote their Two-Spirit members. I cannot find a word in Mohawk that describes me, however, Mohawk is a woman language; if gender is not described in other terms, it is assumed to be female. Perhaps a Two-Spirit was not an *uncommon* enough occurrence to be granted a special word. And perhaps a gay man was known by a female term, and a lesbian like myself was a woman among many other women. I *am* certain that I am not the first Mohawk lesbian to walk this Earth, and that certainty has helped ease the pain I feel when confronted by another Native who discounts me because of my sexuality. I also don't know if all First Nations gave special or exalted status to their Two-Spirit citizens. There are some stories of Two-Spirits being revered *because* of their blurred gender and uncompromising way of living within their clan or tribal unit.[2] These stories are important ones to treasure and repeat to our young, but I think they cannot take the place of living and breathing lesbians and gay men who can be role models if we are able to jump over the chasm that homophobia has blasted into our Nations. And many of us find ourselves at the edge of this precipice separating us from our beloved people.

Those first whitemen who stumbled across our world had no experience in how we thought and believed. They couldn't grasp the concept of peoples living with the sun and moon. Peoples whose time was not measured by hourglasses or clocks, but by what was happening on the earth and in the sky. Peoples who looked at animals to judge when a season was passing and changing. Peoples who acted together, in consensus, because to do otherwise was unthinkable and foolish. Peoples who were not ashamed or afraid of bodily functions or sexual acts. Peoples who had a rhythm that pulsed to that of Earth. The whiteman saw none of this except for the unashamed celebration of sexuality. They were so spellbound, they filled reams of paper on the subject. The Jesuits especially gloried in recounting every sexual act. The Spanish and French wrote home to Europe about the sexual "looseness" of Native women. Of course, these men did not mention the word rape, a common occurrence perpetrated on my women ancestors. Nor did they write back home about our spirituality, except to call us heathens. Neither explorer nor the religious saw our physical presence in *our* own context, nor heard the prayers that were a joyous song to being part of the natural. To this day, the whiteman continues to look at Indigenous Peoples from *their* context, fitting us into *their* limited and limiting view of Earth.

Church and state have long worked as consorts in the colonization of Aboriginal peoples. With the guns came the Bible. With the Bible came the whiskey. With the whiskey came addiction and government over our affairs. With government came reserves, and loathing of all that was natural. With loathing came the unnatural; the internalization of all they told us about ourselves. And the beliefs hold fast in some. There are christian Indians, and there are homophobic Indians. In speaking with an Elder from Tyendinaga, I asked her how things had changed in her ninety-six years of life. She started to cry and said, "We learned all sorts of bad things from the whites. Now we no longer love each other." And perhaps this is the key to understanding homophobia within my Nation. The love that was natural in our world, has become unnatural as we become more consumed by the white world and the values therein. Our sexuality has been colonized, sterilized, whitewashed. Our sense of spirit has been sterilized, colonized, made over to pander to a growing consumer need for quick and easy redemption. What the dominant culture has never been able to comprehend is that spirit/sex/prayer/flesh/religion/natural is who I am as a Two-Spirit. "Now we no longer love each other." What a triumph for the whiteman and the cultural enslavement he brought to the First Nations. When we fight amongst ourselves as to who is a better Indian, who is a more traditional Indian, we are linking arms with the ones who would just as soon see us dead. Homophobia has *no* justification within our Nations.

My partner and I have a small cottage on Walpole Island in Ontario. Walpole Island is held by a confederacy known as the Council of Three Fires — Potawatomi, Ottawa, Ojibwa, and since it comprises several islands, there are numerous canals and tiny channels of water where only a canoe can get through. Denise and I canoe every chance we get. We both love the steady movement of paddles in the water, the sounds of marsh birds, the glimpse of turtles under the water, the sun on our faces, that wondrous smell of fertility all around us, and sometimes the special gift of finding a feather or a nest floating by us. On this one day, we found a small patch of dry land with a black willow growing straight out of the earth. There was a noisy Red-wing flying in and out of the branches. We hesitated before beaching the canoe, knowing how protective these birds are, and not wanting to disturb him or the nest he might be guarding. But he flew away and we climbed out onto the land. We talked, ate our lunch, breathed the air, then lay under the willow and touched each other, kissed, made love between us. As I felt the first tremors of orgasm take hold of me, a Blue Heron entered my body and I became her. Each pulse of orgasm was a flap of wings, a preparation for flight, and as orgasm took hold of me, I felt myself lifting from the ground, wings gathering strength, flying. I opened my long, yellow beak and gave a cry. Later, I asked Denise if she had heard the voice of Heron. "No dearest, I only heard yours."

In this moment of time and place, Heron had chosen me to communicate her cries of freedom, power and joy in being the magnificent creature she is. She told me that her joy was mine and mine was hers. This is physical prayer. This is creation. This is what cannot be stolen from me, or frightened out of me. Although Heron has not come to me again in that special intimate way, when I see her flying, or standing still in water, the long curve of her neck sparkling and shimmering in the sunlight, I feel, once again, the wonder of the great mysteries that are part of the natural order of my world.

Those people who despise sex also despise Heron and others like her. The need to "have dominion over the earth" is not a natural or healthy way to be on Earth. There have been numerous books and articles written by white feminists to describe the hatred of women that is carried over to nature. If men can't kill all women, they will attempt to kill all that lives, especially that which comes from Mother Earth. While I agree with some of this theorizing, I feel it does not encompass Aboriginal thought, or any theories about lesbianism. There is also no mention of enchantment, or to use a better word, *orenda*, a Mohawk description of what cannot be explained but is accepted as the natural order of life.

Perhaps even in feminism it is too difficult to give up a belief in the Eurocentric way of living and being.

A Native man may be sexist, but still lovingly tend corn and beans, say a prayer of forgiveness for killing a deer or moose for his family, and believe fully in the power of magic in his life. I am reminded of a gathering of Native writers that took place in 1992. A Mohawk man gave a speech in which he exhibited the worst kinds of white-leftist haranguing. Some of the women in the audience were angry at his patronizing behaviour and obvious sexism. It was discussed who would speak to him. *I* was selected — because I am Mohawk, because I am his elder by ten or fifteen years. I did speak to him. He listened, albeit, angrily at first. And I knew that this was a man who cared passionately about the environment, about children, who spoke the language of our ancestors, but nevertheless had internalized the European/Marxist thought of male domination, and the macho posturing that comes with it. Sexism is a learned behaviour, not a natural behaviour in Aboriginal cultures. And one can call himself traditional and still be sexist.

The Longhouse religion of recent use comes from the Code of Handsome Lake, or *Gai'wiio'*. Handsome Lake, Seneca Nation, was a reformed alcoholic who had many dreams of a new religion. Born in 1735, in his later years he was terribly aggrieved at the havoc brought to his people by the whiteman. While a man who cared deeply and strongly about his people, Handsome Lake introduced many christian-based concepts and "ways" that he exhorted the People to follow. Among those messages were "marriage" between men and women, the christian concept of adultery and the "forgiveness" of it (if committed by a husband), the disbanding of animal societies and the dances to honour these Totems, the ban against homosexuality, the confessing of witchcraft and the cessation of such practice, the ban on women employing herbs and medicines for the purpose of abortion or birth control. It is interesting to me that witchcraft, as seen by Handsome Lake, was a female activity that involved the seduction of men to perform ugly acts, but the practice of curing and healing was a male activity, thus these practitioners were known as Medicine Men. I find this curiously christian and antithetical to old Iroquois belief, where women held the knowledge of healing and the mysteries of Earth and cosmos.

Before his death in 1815, Handsome Lake carried his message to the People of the Iroquois Confederacy and it has held firm among many of the People. I find nothing traditionally Onkwehonwe in this religion. Homophobia can thrive in the uneasy mixture of christian thought and Aboriginal belief. And it does. If sexism is a learned behaviour, so also is homophobia. They can be un-learned, if the desire is present. Some of the unlearning has to begin with us, the Two-Spirits.

Much of the self-hatred we carry around inside us is centuries old. This self-hatred is so coiled within itself, we often cannot distinguish the racism from the homo-phobia from the sexism. We carry the stories of our grandmothers, our ancestors. And some of these stories are ugly and terrorizing. And some are beautiful testaments to endurance and dignity. We must learn to emulate this kind of testimony. Speaking ourselves out loud — for our people, for ourselves. To deny our sexuality is to deny our part in creation.

The denial of sexuality and of those who live accord-ing to their sexuality is almost unspeakable. It has been named homophobia, but that bland word does not tell of the blasphemous acts committed against us in the name of religion and state. I use the word blasphemy because that is what it is — a defilement of all that is spirit-filled and ceremonial. I also believe that the hatred and violence that is directed against us is a result of the hatred against their god. It must be difficult to follow doctrine that orders them to live perfect, sex-empty, anti-sensual lives, then turn around and behold *us*, the perverts that god also made. This must drive the christians insane with anger. We get away with it and are not punished by this god that exhorts *them* to be good or else! Of course, the more fundamentalist types say AIDS is a punishment. But even this theology is falling by the wayside as more and more heterosexuals and children are being infected. If one hates the god who made them, they can turn that hatred inward and outward to people who are not like them. I have often thought that racism, sexism, homophobia are results of a giant cultural and religious inferiority psychosis. I realize this is not an original theory, but I adhere to the basic premise of it.

Those of us who are Two-Spirit do not believe we are better, smarter, more spiritual or more *Indian* than others. We do not proselytize, promise salvation and redemption, sell amulets or holy cards to a heaven. We do not promise a better life by saving heterosexual souls. We do not tell stories of men dying on crosses to incite guilt. We do live our lives in the best way we can. We do attempt to appreciate the unique position we have in our communities. We are not "just like everybody else." That line is for those who are still trying to prove themselves worthy of the dominant culture's approval.

I think the 1993 March on Washington for "Lesbian,

Gay, and Bi Equal Rights and Liberation" made many mistakes in trying to look and act "just like everybody else." One of the more endearing and daring facets of being gay/lesbian/bi is the outlandishness that permeates our communities. What's wrong with being different from the asexual and conservative culture that actually makes laws about sex and who we do it with?! Why would we want to be accepted by them? Why would we want to be like them? Why the emphasis on the military? Is our main concern that of serving in armies that routinely invade countries that have large populations of people of colour? Is this the agenda we want to be associated with?

During the 1994 celebration and march honouring the twenty-fifth anniversary of the Stonewall riots and the beginning of the gay liberation movement, gay-punks carried signs: stonewall was a riot, not a name brand and your pride = their profits. Instead of turning our gatherings into photo-ops and mainstream-acceptable, capitalist enterprises, we need to *celebrate* our outlaw status in the dominant society and embrace our differences. I'm with the gay-punks. I will not prove myself to anyone. I am a mother — a lesbian mother. I am a grandmother — a lesbian grandmother. I am the lesbian daughter of my mother and father. I am the lesbian lover of women. I am the lesbian partner of Denise. I am the lesbian being who welcomes Heron, Turtle and Moose into my life. I am the lesbian being who prays with words, heart and body. I am a Two-Spirit woman of the Mohawk Nation. I am a lesbian who listens to the spirits who guide me. I am a Two-Spirit who walks this path my ancestors cleared for us. I will not go away; in fact, I will be in-your-face as long as I breathe the air of this life. If I can clear more brush and cut through thickets, I will. For I feel that we also make tradition in our various and varied communities and Nations. This tradition is generous and welcoming. It is a tradition of wholeness and honour. It is a tradition of remembrance and fidelity.

Notes

1. In a conversation with Donna Marchand, Native lesbian writer and student of law, Donna brought up the concept of orgasm as a natural resource. I thank her most gratefully for sharing the brilliance of her mind.
2. See Will Roscoe, *The Zuni Man-Woman* (Albuquerque: University of New Mexico Press, 1991).

Writing as Witness*

Why are the words "Native" and "vision" used together so often? I expect it comes from the place that wishes to ghettoize and confirm our "quaintness" for the dominant culture.

There is a spiritual practice that occurs in many First Nations peoples of venturing out alone to an isolated place to experience a dream, an interaction with spirits, a communion with animal beings *in order to find a life-time path to dwell on.* This practice has been translated into the English language as a "vision quest." Like many Aboriginal words that have been interpreted by the Europeans, "vision quest" hardly begins to explain a complicated religious ceremony that is one of seeking balance and centredness. I suspect that white people consider this "quest" an everyday occurrence for Native peoples because it confirms their view of Natives as "exotic" and more "spiritual" than non-Natives. Like many spiritual practices of First Nations peoples, the idea of vision questing has been "borrowed" by the dominant culture for use in superficial ritual that usually costs money. And the word "vision" is pasted onto anything that concerns Native peoples, as if we are the spiritual

---

* From a panel entitled "Native American Vision," given at Michigan State University, June 1991.

67

nannies of dominant society. It also serves as a way to keep us invisible, except for the occasions when we are trotted out for exhibition as the mood suits the dominant culture. My cultural definition of vision is a vast and far-reaching one. It is also a holy one. I doubt if I have more vision or spirituality than an Irish woman, a Polish woman, an African-American woman. I am a Mohawk woman and my dreams, my beliefs, my vision are *why* I am on the writing path.

In many of my stories there are moments when the protagonist is faced with two choices — to live or to die. Often these choices are brought about because of a circumstance involving the death of a loved one. And this moment of reckoning is brought to the protagonist by a being that is not human. This reckoning is also a reclamation.

Since contact with white people, our battle for survival has not left us free of the internalization of European and christian values. Where death was once viewed as a necessary and natural piece of life's cycle, we often find ourselves in the unnatural state of thinking that death is something to fear or something that we would be better off achieving. "Better dead than Red."

During these five hundred years, the shattering of our cultural and community systems has often led to a split within our individual selves and souls. We want to "forget" all that is Indian, because the remembering is so painful and heartbreaking. This has led to a kind of spiritual malaise or limbo. The erosion of self that accompanies that malaise is another curse of colonialism. We have seen that curse at work in our communities — alcoholism, drug addiction, disrespect for women, incest, suicide, homophobia; these evils are the result of the self-loathing that imperialism has forced into our minds. This is the rape that has left a legacy of unnatural acts in its wake. We are living the testament of that rape every day in our heads. There are times when I am awestruck by the fact that we, as Aboriginal peoples, are still managing to direct our lives and those of our children and grandchildren.

In my story, "Swimming Upstream," the protagonist, Anna May, has come to the reckoning of her life. She has lost her son in a drowning, not through any fault she has committed, but she sees the death of her son as a grievous mistake in a long line of mistakes brought about by her very existence. As a Native woman, a half-breed, a Two-Spirit, she has believed the message of that long-ago *and* present imperative — she deserves to die for the "sins" of being who she is. Anna May chooses to run away from her loving relationship with Catherine, chooses to buy a bottle of wine, "the red, sweet kind that will make her forget," chooses the death that is most familiar to her — alcoholism. What Anna May does not realize, and what I did not realize until *after* I wrote the story, is that Anna May was not acting upon a choice, she was reacting to the encoded rape of her mind by colonization. She was doing what she was supposed to do as a Native — turn death into an ignominious statement, rather than a part of the natural continuum. Anna May was imbalanced, the madness manifested in First Nations people as a result of colonialism.

As I was writing the story, I began to be carried along with Anna May's journey. Instead of directing the events, some other presence started to direct me. I remembered vividly the Bruce Peninsula and the Sauble Falls that contained the hundreds of Salmon who were swimming upstream to spawn. At this point, on the page, Anna May drove her car to that very place I had seen, her bottle of wine unopened in the car. She stopped her car, got out, saw the Salmon, saw the painful, yet beautiful struggle to carry life to new beginnings and new generations. I believe that Salmon was guiding my fingers on the keys. Just as he guided his body and his regeneration into new waters, I was writing with the sounds of water, the sounds of Salmon jumping and flying to get to their mates, to *renew* life, to renew *life*.

As an Indigenous writer, I feel that the gift of writing and the *privilege* of writing holds a responsibility to be a witness to my people. To be a witness of the natural world, to be a witness to Salmon, to Anna May, to her son, to the sometimes unbearable circumstances of our lives. Anna May's "choice" to relive the pain that would lead to death — alcohol — was stopped by the power and magic of Salmon. Her vision of death is turned upon itself. She is directed by the natural, the Indigenous, the real. She sees her son in the water, swimming to another way of being, another place, a place she cannot enter with dishonour. Thus, Anna May makes a real choice. She turns her car around and proceeds back home. She will begin the slow process of healing her mind. She will throw away the old messages, the old codes. She will make new ones, for herself, for her people. At least, this is what I think, for by now, Anna May is not just a protagonist in a story, she is a real being in my life. Salmon has not only given me his story, he has given me hers. And when I read this story aloud to groups of people, so many come to me after and tell me that this is their story also. And so many Native people speak to me of their renewal, their choice to be a witness to our history.

In another story, "This Place," David, a young gay Native, returns to his Reserve to die. He has lived in the city for much of his adult life, and comes home because he has AIDS and wants to be among his people and on his land for the act of death. Yet David fears death. He is terrorized by what he does not know, or rather, what he does not "remember." David left the Reserve feeling he did not belong because of his homosexuality. And while he has not given up his Nativehood in the city, he has put parts of himself aside in order to survive. David has large amounts of anger towards his people for the homophobia he perceives, and large amounts of anger towards the white, gay, male community he knows to be racist. His mother calls in a medicine man, Joseph, to help David reconcile his life *and* death. Joseph brings many things with him, a piece of mirror, a feather from a Whistling Swan, a document written by David's ancestor, a snake skin, and a cat. This cat, The Prophet, named after the great Shawnee warrior, is the means through which David sees death as one of the many parts of the whole. Joseph, who is also gay, takes David on many journeys, gathering up the pieces that David lost or cast aside in his struggle to be a gay Native man in a white world that despises both. The homophobia that David perceives in his people is not imagined. As First Nations people, our spiritual loss includes the dishonouring of our gay and lesbian citizens. This painful rebuff leads many of us to leave our ancestral lands to look for support elsewhere. For many of us, this meant large cities, seeking others who shared a like sexuality, perhaps even finding a kind of anonymity. We were anathematized, or at least, made to feel like we were a curse to our own people. David was also imbalanced. Like Anna May, the effects of colonial domination had seeped into his mind, his heart. Thus, his fear of facing death, a fear he "knew" was required of him.

I am also a respectful admirer of Cat. I do not think she is "cute" nor do I think of her as a pet. She is distinguished and elegant. Brilliant and knowing. Wise and very, very old. Her insistence and persistence (I am only human and it takes me longer to "get it") brought much of this story to fruition. It is no coincidence that my beloved Maggie sat in my room during the writing of this story, grooming herself, watching me with her green eyes, occasionally walking across my keyboard to keep me in line.

While writing this story, I thought about many of the Native gay men I have met. Some are in the Spirit World, some are living with AIDS on Reserves and in cities. Some are HIV negative, some have just been diagnosed. All are courageous and lovely. David is all of them, and he is also the Native man who fears the natural process of death. Some of us are not fortunate enough to have a holy person, a shaman to guide our feelings and spirits through the many labyrinths and mysteries we call death. The great act of remembering *who we are* can bring acceptance of the Mystery.

What I want to say is this. Vision is not just a perception of what is possible, it is a window to the knowledge of what *has* happened and what *is* happening. Our side of the window shows some unlovely and frightening acts that, for us, the Indigenous peoples of this continent, continue to be re-enacted. But there is a crack in the window that allows us the real view, the natural state of being. It is through this crack that our writers slip the stories, the words, sending them out to be ignored, burned, or found and cherished, carried along by the wind, by a bird, by a woman who retells the stories to her young. This is our tradition. Our words *are* the vision, given with generosity and hope. There is nothing "quaint" in this.

From E. Pauline Johnson to Nicole Tanguay, our words and stories have undergone numerous transfigurations. What we once *told* is now being *written*. The legacy of our community rape is being transformed into a new legacy of hope, truth and self-love. I feel my own work has changed and renewed itself: has lived, has died, has lived — will die again, will live again. There was a time when I believed and even said out loud that I was not a writer any longer. I was in thrall to self-loathing, to the false legacy, to the unnatural. It is no coincidence that during that time I didn't hear the birds' singing, I didn't see the seeds making themselves over into corn, I didn't feel the love that was being sent to me. I had ceased to think Mohawk. I was a victim of the message. Though I managed to crawl, to dog-paddle out of that abyss, it would not have been possible if the natural world had not insisted itself upon me. I was overwhelmed with sensations of higher beings. I saw a Yellow-Headed Blackbird, stopping in the Midwest before continuing on to the West. Blue Herons appeared everywhere. I smelled grass. I heard corn growing. I felt love and its effect on my body through orgasm. I became Mohawk again. I became me again. The abundance of Earth's messages drowned out the un-Earthly message. Story gave itself to me. I began to write again.

We have been forced to reject and thereby forget what

has made us real as Native peoples. The dominant society longs for this forgetfulness on our part. It hungers for our assimilation into their world, their beliefs, their code. And it hurries this process along by promises of acceptance and forgiveness. Their paranoia threatens to become our own. But what we may have "forgotten" is still in our blood. Salmon's desire to go home is our desire also. Blue Heron's desire to fly long distances to make a home is ours also. Corn's desire to grow is ours also. For we are parts of them and they are parts of us. This is why we are Indigenous. This is what none of us *has* truly forgotten, though the false message pounds and thrashes our minds. Who we are is written on our bodies, our hearts, our souls. This is what it means to be Native in the dawn of the twenty-first century. Witness to what has been and what is to be. Knowing what has transpired and dreaming of what will come. Listening to the stories brought to us by other beings. Renewing ourselves in the midst of chaos.

May Salmon's story always be carried in our blood. May David's story be remembered with honour. This is my vision and hope. This is why I write.

To Be or Not To Be Has Never Been the Question

My first work was published in 1981, the year I turned forty and the year I began writing. By first work I mean just that — the first pieces of writing I had ever done. I was not a journal-keeper or one to write down thoughts or feelings. I lived my life, I talked my stories to friends, to lovers, to family. This was the way it was.

Then I saw Eagle. He swooped in front of our car as Denise and I were driving through Iroquois land. He wanted us to stop and so we did. I got out of the car and faced him as he sat on a branch of a White Pine, his wings folded gracefully, his magnificent head gleaming in the October afternoon sun. We looked into each other's eyes. I was marked by him. I remember that I felt transported to another place, perhaps another time. We looked into each other for minutes, maybe hours, maybe a thousand years. I had received a message, a gift. When I got home I began to write.

Sinister Wisdom was my first publisher, the feminist journal produced at that time by Michelle Cliff and Adrienne Rich. The two pieces I submitted, "Mohawk Trail" and "Native Origin," were raw and unformed.

Michelle wrote me a letter and in a few sentences helped me with the forming. The rawness I wanted to keep. Perhaps because to me, rawness was synonymous with honesty. And I believed, and still believe, that honesty is what writing is about. Was this work lesbian-identified? Yes, because that's who I am. In my bio I stated very clearly and proudly — I am a Mohawk lesbian. These two identities are parts of who I am. I have felt in these years I have been writing, that betraying who *I* am would be a betrayal of the grandmothers and sisters who came before me. And it would be a betrayal of the daughters and granddaughters who are to follow me. This is not altruistic — it is Native. It is not naive — it is Mohawk. Eagle brought that gift to me, *to the me I am.*

In the Native community we believe that questioning self-identity is indulged in by white people who spend time agonizing, using up breathable air discussing this subject. In other words, self-identity crises are an exercise for those who have no community or history of that community. We're all Native, so what is good for one will ultimately benefit the community. That's what I was taught. Yet, I have been hurt and ostracized by some Natives, men and women, who have made it clear that being a lesbian, or *saying* it out loud is not good for our community. I believe what they are really saying is — you embarrass me with your sexuality, therefore you embarrass our people, and *white* people will have even more ammunition to use against us. I do not mean to imply that my people are looking for approval from the dominant society. But some individuals may be invested in the dominant culture — whether it be a good job, or dependency on government funds, or having a place in literary circles, or an internalized belief in the stereotype of what First Nations women should be — and are frightened by what can be taken away. And why shouldn't they be? Everything else has been stolen, why not the small niches that keep a roof over our heads and food on our tables? Yet, I want to say that homophobia is the eldest son of racism and one does not exist without the other. Our community suffers from both — externally and internally.

If I have been shunned by some heterosexual Natives, I have been moved and energized by others. I gave a reading at a university and in the audience was an Elder, a Yankton Sioux woman who I greatly admire and respect for her work in getting Indian skeletal remains removed from museums and rightfully returned to their people for proper and honoured burial. I was awed to be in the same room with her and very nervous about reading the story I had planned, one about a lesbian mother whose son has died. I began telling my story, finding, as I do, that I was drawn into the words, the telling, forgetting the external world. After the reading, the Elder, a big, commanding woman, came up to me. She touched the necklace I was wearing, "Very impressive," she said. Then she smiled, "You sure write purty." I took her hand and said, "Thank you Grandmother." Later I fled to a quiet place to have a cigarette and a cry. *She liked the way I told a story.* Surely, the finest praise I could receive. *These* kinds of encounters have happened much more frequently than the other hurtful kind.

And yet...and yet, I earn my living by my writing. That Elder cannot, by herself, pay the mortgage and feed my stomach, though her words fed my Native writer's soul. There comes a time when I can't ignore being ignored by those whose reviews would mean the difference between getting royalties on a hundred books or ten thousand. I *would* prefer the ten thousand, there is no doubt of that! But what would that mean? Do I really want my work reviewed in the *New York Times Book Review?* Sometimes, yes. Although, knowing how the system works and who is controlling the system, I would no doubt be reviewed by some whiteman who once wrote a half-assed article about Natives and is therefore the resident "expert." His opinion doesn't matter to me or to most of my people. Take this quote from *Booklist*, a review catalogue sent out to booksellers in the U.S.: "Beth Brant's book, *Mohawk Trail* is impossible to classify simply." The review ends by saying "Highly recommended for Native American literature collections," but leaves out the fact that I am lesbian, I am urban, I am Mohawk. Instead I am described as "part Indian." True enough that I am a half-breed; a lot of my work centres on that state of being, or as LeAnne Howe, Choctaw writer puts it, "You're torn between wanting to kill everyone in the room, or buyin' 'em all another round of drinks." I imagine the reviewer couldn't classify my writing (why does an act of creation *have* to be classified?) because I don't write in stereotypes and I write about queers.

Frankly, there have been fewer reviews of my books in the feminist press than in mainstream publications. *Mohawk Trail* was reviewed in one feminist newspaper, *Sojourner*, and that review was written by Joy Harjo, someone hard to ignore. The review was wonderful, not because of the good things she had to say about my writing, but because she *knew* where I was coming from. The feminist press must subscribe to the theory (or the wish) held dear by the dominant culture — all Natives are dead and gone except for a few "quaint" representatives that usually reside somewhere "out there in the Southwest. You know, the kind that Tony Hillerman writes about." I am never asked to do reviews of Native writers' books by feminist publications. And this is where I really get enraged. I have been a working, marching, demonstrating participant in the women's movement for almost thirty years, steadfast in my belief that feminism is the saving grace for peoples — women, men, children, and those beings of the air, the sea, the land, and the cosmos. Native women's books are *rarely* reviewed in the feminist media, but I notice that Lynn Andrew's books and others of that ilk are steady best-sellers in the women's bookstores that still carry them. I have never been a civil-rights feminist. I believe, as Audre Lorde wrote, "The master's tools will never dismantle the master's house." Writing for the masters and Miss Ann's of the house will not be the tool that destroys racism. I would like to be reviewed in my many complexities as a human being — mother, grandmother, Mohawk, lesbian, feminist, working-class, mammal and on and on.

One of the best reviews I received was written by a white, gay man. The review came from a working-class perspective and from a man who understood the conflicts and triumphs of being gay. I realized, with that review, that no one discusses the issue of class in the same breath with Native writers. Just as we are perceived to live somewhere "out there," we are never considered to be workers, and never is it mentioned what we have to endure to bring a pay cheque home. My dad worked on the line putting parts on cars. He also painted houses, worked in a salt mine, worked construction, planted trees during the Depression, bartered physical labour for venison. This is where I come from — an urban Indian, working-class home. We were poor sometimes, but Daddy *always* worked and so did Mom. Sometimes, being a writer, I feel like I'm not *really* working. But I appreciate the lessons my mom and dad taught me about hard work. My working-class history gives me a sure nose for pretension, especially in myself. I can spot a phoney a mile away. I like that about myself.

I accept that writing is a gift brought to me. And being a writer is not a separate entity from the rest of me. Because it is a gift, a constant interchange takes place. When the writing spirits call me (I do not write every day, although I *think* about writing every day), I respond. My body responds, my heart responds, my racial memory responds. I do not censor myself when writing. I will not make a character heterosexual if she or he is not. In sending out my vitae I will not excise those anthologies or journals that have the words lesbian, gay, dyke or queer in them. I may as well excise those journals and anthologies that have the words Native, Indian or woman in their titles. In my bio notes I usually say I am a Mohawk lesbian mother and grandmother. It is fascinating to see who will accept my work and what they will do with it and me. Editors who wouldn't change my stories without permission, feel they can change the contents of my bio. Suddenly I find myself a mother and grandmother who lives in the States! These omissions used to anger me; now I find them oddly amusing. I figure by now most readers know me as "that Mohawk lesbian," or "that nice Indian Granny who lives in the States." Both statements are true. And *I* know who I am — something I couldn't have said years ago when I was a battered woman, a self-hating half-breed, a woman who self-destructed at every turning, before I acknowledged my lesbianism and before I began to write. Anyway, most of my stories are about lesbians and gay men; all are about Indians.

It would be an untruth to say that coming out as a lesbian set me free. But it is a truth that writing put me on a path towards freedom. I don't mean personal freedom. I mean freedom to be a loving and useful member of my Nation and my communities. I have used this analogy before, but I will use it again here — the Sun Dance. The Sun Dance is a ceremony of Plains Indians where the participant endures hours and even days of dancing into the sun to make a communion with Creator. While to white-European eyes it may seem a dance of the individual, in reality it is a dance for the People. I never felt this so forcefully as when I was editing *A Gathering of Spirit*. Each Native woman who contributed to the anthology was making her dance. All of us, together, made a dance for each other. Our community. Our communion. This is how I feel when I am writing and the spirits are singing to me. I am making communion with my people, with Creator, with myself — all those pieces becoming one. All working together. All dancing and feasting together. It is *why* I write. To make a whole. To take these splits forced on us by racism, classism, homophobia, colourism, and baste them together. To weave a cloth that holds our dreams and story.

Through the years this cloth has become stronger and that is due to the many Two-Spirits I have met and with whom I have corresponded. These brothers and sisters have helped hold me together. My giveaway to them is to be a stronger writer and member of our family. I do not write out of isolation or a longing for the Muse — that European entity that mysteriously appears to white men. I have chosen solitude for myself. The room where

I work is a hermitage of sorts. But I am never alone here. My senses are fired up and ready to transmit and to receive. There may be music — from Lou Reed to Kiri Te Kanawa. There are pictures on my wall — from grandsons to friends to family. There are objects to touch — a piece of old brick found at a Mission graveyard, a pine cone that reminds me of a time when a lover and I made love on the earth. There is tobacco and sage burning to please the spirits. My candles are lit to remind me of the fires of my people. I am not alone here.

Native peoples have always told story. Among those storytellers were Two-Spirits. This I know, despite the attempts of Jesuits, missionaries and other infiltrators to "whitewash" us and make us invisible, even to ourselves. I am continuing an old tradition, only this time around using a computer. Story is meant to be spoken — that has not changed. The written becomes the spoken whether by hands or mouth, the spoken enters the heart, the heart turns over, Earth is renewed. In the end, this is what matters to me. "I write because to not write is a breach of faith." I believe that now as surely as I did in 1984 when I wrote those words. I must have faith in the power of a Mohawk lesbian to make a difference through writing. I have faith in the power of Native Two-Spirits to make that difference through beading and weaving words into life. We do our work with love.

Grandmothers of a New World

Pocahontas and Nancy Ward hold a special fascination for me because of the legends that have arisen around their names and lives. They are presented, by white historians, as good friends of the whiteman, helping colonialists gain a foot-hold in Indian Country. At the same time, some Natives have used the word "traitor" to describe them. Deified and vilified. Somewhere outside their legends the truth lies. As a poet, rather than a historian, I feel I have a freedom of sorts to explore and imagine what those truths are.

According to "history," Pocahontas was a favoured daughter of Wahunsonacock ("Powhatan"), chief of the Algonquian Confederacy in what is now called Virginia. In 1607 or 1608 she saw her first whiteman, John Smith, on a ship sailing into the harbour. She immediately became enamoured of his colour and promptly fell in love with him. Wahunsonacock, being the "savage" he was, hated John Smith and for no apparent reason gave the order to have him executed. Right before he was to be tomahawked, Pocahontas threw herself on Smith, telling her father that he'd have to kill her too. Since Pocahontas was willing to die for this particular whiteman, there must be something wonderful about all white men, so Wahunsonacock spared not only Smith's life but the lives of his crew as well.

Smith eventually returned to England, leaving Pocahontas to pine away until she met John Rolfe. Pocahontas must have thought that all white men looked alike, or maybe she liked the name John, because she enthusiastically fell in love with Rolfe and became a good christian. She also became a good capitalist since she helped her husband grow rich in the tobacco trade, took up wearing white women's clothing, had a son, went to England where she was a celebrity, and finally died happily there — her soul eternally saved.

Quite a story. Even Hollywood couldn't improve this tale.

But I can.

Wahunsonacock had twenty children, ten of them daughters. Pocahontas was a favoured daughter, but more than that, was a child in her father's confidence. She understood only too well what the invasion of Europeans meant for her people. I also must tell you that at the time she met John Smith, she was twelve or thirteen — a woman by Native standards of the day. Pocahontas was not just a good listener, she was listened to. When she spoke, the Pamunkey people heard her and respected her voice. While not a true matriarchy like the Mohawk of Molly Brant or the Cherokee of Nanye'hi (Nancy Ward), Pamunkey women held sway in the disposition of enemy warriors and matters pertaining to war. John Smith's so-called rescue was, in fact, a mock execution — a traditional ritual often held after the capture of enemies. This ritual, in the eyes of John Smith, must have held all the trappings of a play with Smith in the starring role. Pocahontas also played her part. She chose to adopt Smith as her brother since this was her right as a Pamunkey woman. Smith began writing letters home of how his life was saved by a genuine Indian princess, and of how he held the Algonquian Confederacy in the palm of his hand. Of course, this was nonsense.

Wahunsonacock and his daughter/confidante were not fools. They had a sophisticated view of the English and the other European nations who were clamouring to capture the "new" continent and claim it for their own. The continuation of their people was uppermost in the daughter's and father's minds. They thought to establish their Nation by making alliances with the British. Then, as now, survival was the most important thought on Native agendas. The art and practice of diplomacy was not a new concept to North American Native peoples. If we were as savage and warlike as the history books would like us to believe, there would not have been any of us left when the first whiteman staggered onto our lands. Pocahontas was probably the first ambassador to the British, just as La Malinche was to the Spanish. Not an easy task for anyone, let alone a thirteen-year-old woman who could not read, write, or speak the language of the intruders, and who most likely figured out early on that the British held little esteem for women — especially if they weren't white. Pocahontas saw as the alternative to genocide, adopting Smith as her brother.

History books speculate on whether Smith and Pocahontas were lovers. I doubt this is important, but "history," intent on romanticizing Pocahontas and Smith, seems to linger on this attachment. I think that "history" is a lie — written down to bolster the ego of the whiteman, to promulgate their status as macho and clever warriors, *and* the ludicrous idea that whitemen are irresistible to Native women. Boastful and self-involved, John Smith eventually left the Jamestown Colony and went home to England. He hadn't made his fortune, but he was to make a mark in books to come through his lies and distortions of Aboriginal peoples.

There are reports that Pocahontas and her father were greatly angered at Smith's leave-taking. Why? Did they see it as a withdrawal of agreement made between Great Britain and the Algonquian Confederacy? Through Smith's adoption, they had woven a tenuous connection between the Nations. The Algonquian Confederacy had lost few people to these British invaders. The Confederacy was still strong in the eyes of other First Nations. They were not weakened by their relationship with the British, due to the diplomatic skills of Wahunsonacock and Pocahontas. The British had done fairly well in the Colony. Natives taught them what to eat, how to eat, how to plant what they ate. It amazes me how Thanksgiving in the States is portrayed as whites and Natives happily sharing food in a gesture of friendship. The pilgrims had nothing to share. Suspicious and ignorant of new kinds of food, as well as Native peoples, it is a wonder to me that any of them survived at all. But we were generous — a generosity that became the beginning of the end of our cultures as we knew them. My eldest grandsons are righteously appalled when Thanksgiving is celebrated in their schools. "Teacher, the pilgrims were bad guys. They killed Indians!" Of course, "teacher" continues to perpetuate this mythical holiday as a story where the whiteman is the good guy, feeding the starving Natives! When *will* they get it right?

In Aboriginal languages, there are no words for stingy or selfish, except to describe aberrant behaviour requiring a shaman's intervention. Our generosity comes from the complex and sophisticated worldview of thousands of years of belief and practice. The concept of family is a wide and far-reaching part of our worldview. By adopting John Smith as her brother, Pocahontas was opening her home and family to him. Smith violated this honour and the meaning of family by leaving Jamestown without a proper goodbye and thank you. This violation brought humiliation to the family, clan and Nation. As a result of Smith's behaviour, Wahunsonacock and Pocahontas left the Jamestown settlement and went home, enjoining other Natives to follow them. Jamestown suffered heavy losses of life. They literally starved. Pocahontas was sent on various missions to other Nations by her father. Serving as a spokesperson for the Algonquian Confederacy, she arranged new trade agreements, cemented old friendships, built new ones. There is no doubt that Pocahontas was a skilled orator and politician. It sickens me that the story we learn in school is the racist and untrue depiction of her romance with John Smith, and her willingness to die for him.

During her travels, Pocahontas took a Native husband. Of him, we can find no trace. She must not have had children, or they would have remained with their mother on her sojourns and her eventual return to her home and family. When Wahunsonacock and Pocahontas were ready to visit Jamestown again (to see what the whiteman was up to), they were taken prisoner. I imagine settlers wanted to vent their anger on them for being deserted. It would never have occurred to the pilgrims that their own racism and stupidity had led to this "desertion" and ultimate loss of lives. Pocahontas and her father were not free to leave the colony, but could wander among the people and houses. They found a man who must have intrigued them to no end. He was a missionary and was teaching people to read and write. Reading was something the whiteman did, and because of it, he held a certain kind of power. Bargaining with the British, Pocahontas arranged for her father to be sent home and she would stay to learn more about the christian way. "History" says Pocahontas was an eager convert. I submit that her conversion to christianity was only half-hearted, but her conversion to literacy was carried out with powerful zeal.

I feel in my heart that Pocahontas was guided by divine power. Not a god in christian terms, but a communion with Creator. "Living with the spirits," as my father used to say. Pocahontas lived with and listened to these spirits. There is a term and philosophy that has been used for centuries — Manifest Destiny. It is a whiteman's term and logic implying that whites are superior and therefore, it is Nature's law that the white race hold dominion over all natural things. In other words, the whiteman is king and emperor over all — Indigenous peoples, animals, plants, the very air. I propose that Pocahontas had her own destiny to fulfil — that of keeping her people alive. Would Wahunsonacock and his people have listened and learned so readily from Pocahontas if she had not already given evidence of being a person who "lived with the spirits?" Was Pocahontas a shaman, a seer, a holy woman? In some English translations of her name, it appears to come up as "getting joy from spirits." Name-giving in Native cultures is a serious event. Many signs and omens are consulted before giving a name and getting a name. In many Nations, it was the role of the berdache, or Two-Spirit, to bestow this honour.

History will not tell us that Pocahontas was a holy woman, but there is a feeling inside me that tells me this is so. I know my feeling cannot be substantiated by an academic literature; but I am not a member of the academy, nor am I a scholar of institutions — I am a Mohawk woman storyteller who knows there were and are prophets among my people. Pocahontas was such a prophet who lived her prophecy.

Linda Hogan, Chickasaw poet, has written letters to me about the "New People." These are people like her and me — the mixed-bloods. Did Pocahontas envision Nations of New People? Did she vision a New World? A world where people would say, "I am a human being of many races and Nations." Is this the real destiny? Vine Deloria once said, "Blood quantums are not important; what really matters is who your grandparents were." These women I am writing about were our grandparents. They are our Grandmothers in spirit, if not actual blood. This does not mean that I think every person who dwells on this continent is a spiritual Indian. That would be a dishonour to my ancestors. I emphatically believe that our culture and ritual belong to us — First Nations. A person does not become an Indian by participating in a sweat, or observing a Sun Dance, or even working on political issues that affect our Nations. One cannot choose to be Indigenous like one chooses new clothes or chooses a brand of toothpaste. One is not Indigenous because they believe in our values. But the prophecy of New People *can* mean the beginning of a different kind of discourse between Nations and races.

While learning to read and write, Pocahontas met John Rolfe. The accounts come down through time that he greatly admired her. He may indeed have admired her.

She was a powerful voice in the territory; she held great wealth of land; she knew the many secrets of growing tobacco which Rolfe had come to realize could make him a rich man. Rolfe came from gentry stock, but was fairly poor compared to others of his class. Why else would he have come to the continent, except in search of untold wealth, just waiting for him to take? "History" tells us that Rolfe was taken with Pocahontas because of her "regal bearing, her christian demeanor, her wisdom." All this may be true and perhaps even love entered into it. Did Pocahontas love John Rolfe? Maybe. Did the spirits tell her that Rolfe was a good choice to begin the prophecy? There were other whitemen waiting in the wings to know the favours of Pocahontas and her father, for one was not possible without the other. John Rolfe was a man easily handled by those who had more charisma and political savvy than he. And he was not ugly. The courtship began, but not without obstacles. The court of King James was very adamant in discouraging contact between the races (although I doubt there was discouragement against rape and pillage). The issue of class was a barrier to the marriage. This is why we end up with the ridiculous legends of Pocahontas being a princess. John Smith had started the flame of this particular bonfire when he wrote home about having his life saved by a princess of the realm. John Rolfe added more fuel to the legend in his desire to be married. Thus Wahunsonacock is made a king and Pocahontas a princess. In reality, kings and princesses — royalty — do not exist and never have existed in our cultures.

Of a dowry there is no mention, but it would be fair to speculate that Rolfe received a parcel of land on which to experiment with tobacco. The smoking of tobacco was a great hit in England among the royals. King James was said to disapprove of the habit, but it doesn't appear that too many people paid attention to what he had to say. Queen Anne was addicted to the stuff and she and her ladies-in-waiting spent hours smoking tobacco and requesting more.

The myth of Pocahontas wants us to believe that after marrying Rolfe, she quickly became a lady of leisure, even acquiring the name of Rebecca. I find this choice of names intriguing and prophetic. In Pocahontas' quest for literacy, the Bible was the only tool she had at that time. Did she read the story of another ancient legend, Rebecca, who was told "Be thou the mother of thousands of millions, and let thy seed possess the gate of those which hate them." When Pocahontas found herself pregnant did she feel the joy of having a child of her prophecy? A child of mixed-blood who would learn to read and write as a matter of course, while inheriting the wisdom, political skills and rich culture of his mother?

To ensure that this child would come into the best of all worlds, Pocahontas surrounded herself with female relatives and her father. John Rolfe may have been alarmed that Lady Rebecca was choosing to have her child in what he considered a primitive and heathen manner, but, then again, maybe he wasn't. We do know that in 1615, Pocahontas gave birth to a son amidst the chanting and singing of her people. So much for Pocahontas' christian submissiveness. After the birth, the relatives stayed on. Unlike John Smith, Rolfe seemed to recognize the honour of being part of Pocahontas' family. When a non-Native becomes part of a Native household or family group, whether through marriage or companionship, the Native family takes over. This is assimilation of a kind that is never discussed or written about. The non-Native often has to put up small battles to hang on to a separate personality rather than the personality of the Native group.

I have seen this happen in my own family with my non-Native uncles, mother and my lover. Soon they are talking like Natives, joking like Natives; the prevailing Native culture and worldview is assimilated by the non-Native. I suspect this process is not discussed because the dominant culture does not want to admit that another way of *seeing* may be a more integrated way of being in the world, as opposed to Manifest Destiny. Again, this process of assimilation is *not* becoming Indigenous. It is a recognition that every part of what constitutes life, *makes life*.

This integrity of life can be explained through the example of the Sun Dance of Plains Indians. Each person entering the circle to dance has an objective. Whether he or she is dancing for strength, for healing the body and/or mind, that purpose will be reflected on the community, for the good of community. In Oklahoma a few years ago, a Vietnam veteran asked to participate in the Sun Dance while using his wheelchair. This had never been done, but a way was worked out where a guide would maneuver him through the rigorous ceremony. This was not an easy task for veteran or guide. The Sun Dance can last for hours; it has been known to last for days until communion with Creator has taken place. Later, when the Dance was done, the vet told a friend of mine that he was dancing to be forgiven for the "sins" (his word) he had committed in Vietnam. As he was dancing, he began to relive his experiences in' Vietnam; he began dancing for his buddies, dancing for the Vietnamese people, he began dancing for peace and the end to racism, he began dancing for the spiritual health that would bring him home to his own people again. This story has everything to do with Pocahontas and her prophecy. While not belonging to the Plains worldview that produces a Sun Dance, Pocahontas was doing her own dance for the good of the community. Her community, because of the child she bore, was an enlarged one. And I am wondering if John Rolfe's idea of family and community was also enlarged.

Pocahontas and Rolfe were invited to England to be presented to the king and queen. The tobacco industry was a profitable one to the monarchy. They wanted to meet Pocahontas, the "princess" of the Indians. Natives were becoming the rage in England. Natives were "in." To this day, Natives remain an object of fascination to European people. Perhaps they are fascinated by the fact that we still exist after five hundred years of persistent genocide. North Americans are not much better — to them we are invisible, extinct, or relics of a past ("primitive") way of life.

The England of the 1600s was a primitive, filthy place and must have been a terrifying sight to Pocahontas and her relatives. For she did not travel to London with just her husband and son, she took many female relatives and her uncle, Uttamatamakin, a medicine man to her people. It has been recorded that while in London, Pocahontas and her Native relatives swam daily in the waters of the Thames. This was seen as a heathen aberration by the British who were accustomed to taking baths perhaps once or twice a year. Some of Pocahontas' relatives became ill from the polluted waters and had to stop their "savage" habit of bathing daily.

Pocahontas met the king and queen. It is reported that

they were impressed. We have no account that Pocahontas reciprocated the feeling. And this leads to another question — where are Pocahontas' writings? We know she could read and write in English; does it not seem likely that she kept a diary or journal of the events in which she was participating? Illness made inroads into the health of the Native people. John Rolfe got permission to take the family to the country where the air and waters were cleaner. Thomas, the son, could play and Pocahontas and her relatives could relax away from the rude stares and comments that followed them everywhere. Pocahontas also met up with her old acquaintance/brother, John Smith. He wrote in his diary that the princess seemed angry with him. He was probably quite angry himself. The reception accorded Pocahontas and Rolfe must have rankled him. The "princess" of his making was truly being treated as royalty.

Pocahontas fell ill. She had already lost some of her people to England's diseases and had spent her time in the country in mourning. Thomas was also ill, which must have sent his mother into a frenzy of trying to get him away from a country that did nothing but kill her people. Rolfe and Pocahontas prepared to take their leave and go home. They set sail; but in Gravesend, in the county of Kent, the ship had to stop and Pocahontas was removed to receive medical care. Perhaps she had tuberculosis or smallpox. Uttamatamakin performed healing rituals for her. This may have been enough to ease her mind and spirit, but British doctors came, and over the protestations of her relatives, applied leeches and gave her purges. This weakened her further. Pocahontas died and her last reported words were, "It is enough that the child liveth." John Rolfe, a weak man without Pocahontas' intervention, failed her in death, since he had her buried christian-style. Uttamatamakin was furious and the anti-white feelings that were held at bay during Wahunsonacock's tenure began stirring and set the scene for hard times to come in Virginia.

Why did Rolfe fail Pocahontas? It may be due to the fact that his son was still very sick and he wanted to leave for Virginia as soon as possible. Rolfe may have chosen the most politically expedient way to placate his British hosts. Pocahontas was no longer there to strengthen him. Or perhaps John Rolfe was always a fool, believing that the Brit way was the only way. Pocahontas' relatives were token christians as she was, and probably would have gone along with a christian burial *if* they also could send her to the Spirit World through Pamunkey ministrations. But Pocahontas was interred at Gravesend in full English dress and tradition; her body remains there to this day.

Wahunsonacock died within a short time after receiving news of his daughter's death. He longed to stay alive to take his grandson to live with him. He must have mourned and longed himself to death. His beloved daughter would never come home again. Her bones would nourish British land instead of her own. And the precious child Thomas, so important to Pocahontas' vision of a new world? He stayed in England and was reared by his father's uncle. John Rolfe went back to Virginia and died shortly after the Native uprising. This foolish, weak man who failed his wife's dream, failed all of us. As a teen, Thomas did return to Virginia and experienced the desire to see his mother's land and the place he first drew breath. He journeyed to the Pamunkey, which was considered enemy territory by the British. What happened to Thomas as he journeyed to the land and language of his birth? A few years later, he was commissioned as a lieutenant in the colonial militia and took up duty as a colonist against the Native people. The so-called Peace of Pocahontas was at an end. Had his mother lived, would the outcome have been different? It is hard to speculate. La Malinche lived to see her son by Cortez take up arms against her people and his. The Pamunkey people and those of many other Nations were on a path to extinction through the Europeans' greatest weapon — disease. It is estimated by Native historians that two-thirds of Indigenous North Americans were wiped out by measles, chicken pox, tuberculosis, smallpox and the common cold. Did Pocahontas see this in her vision?

It is ironic and horrible that Pocahontas became grandmother to an estimated two million people who lay claim to being her descendants. Ironic, because a Virginian who would recoil in horror at having a Black ancestor, points with pride to the Native blood in his body. Horrible, because the British did their job well — anointing Pocahontas a princess, while excising her Native blood. We are left with the legend of a woman made into an "incidental" Indian. There was nothing incidental about Pocahontas. She fought for her people and for the future of her people. She spoke in her own language even at the end. She brought her son into the world through Native womb and hands. Even her final words — "It is enough the child liveth," speaks volumes of her plan. The false European legend must end. Pocahontas' honour demands it.

Nancy Ward was also a woman committed to vision. Her name Nanye'hi, "Spirit People" or "Spirit Path," describes communion with a dream that gave direction to her life and that of her people, the Cherokee Nation.

Nanye'hi became the wife of Kingfisher in 1750 and the stories about her begin at that time. While a mother of two young children, she went into battle with her husband to fight the Creek, traditional enemies of the Cherokee. The Cherokee Nation was a true matriarchy, meaning the blood lines flowed through the mother. Clans of the mother became the clans of the children. Women influenced all political and family matters. Accompanying her mate into battle was not a new phenomenon to the Cherokee. While in what is now called Georgia, Nanye'hi took up the arms of her husband who lay dying, and continued to fight and rally the people around her. This inspiration led her people into ultimate victory over the Creek Nation. Stories began to circulate among the Cherokee about Nanye'hi's heroism. She soon was chosen to become a Beloved Woman of the Cherokee. Beloved Woman means just that; she was beloved by the people, but even more, was beloved by Creator and was a conduit through which Creator spoke.

It seems that only Indigenous people could come up with this particular way of being and seeing. Most of us know some stories of christian saints who supposedly were in communication with a god, but Native peoples so cherish and personalize Creator and the spirits who make the mysteries that this Great Mystery chooses to speak through women's voices. This is not unique only to the Cherokee. Across North America one will hear the voices of women speaking from the spirits. Again, I think of christian women saints who had to be martyred and *die* before achieving the state of grace their religion told them they didn't have in life. How much more sensible to be in a state of grace as a living human.

When Nanye'hi became a Beloved Woman, the Cherokee

97

were literally caught in the middle between France and England. Each European nation was panting and scheming for Cherokee land and it fell on Nanye'hi to negotiate with each nation while retaining and preserving the integrity and strength of her own Nation. Like Pocahontas, she was a diplomat of skillful means. She worked in close connection with her uncle, Attakullakulla, maintaining a balance of power. Imagine it — young woman, aging man, holding war at bay, gathering strength to withstand the onslaught they knew would eventually come. Because she maintained this balance and peace, Nanye'hi has been seen by some of her descendants as a traitor and lackey to the British. But this story is old and familiar. Take strong Nationalist women and turn them into pale myth. Make *our own people* believe the lies. This is what oppression is — the enforcement of amnesia — to make us forget the glory and story of our own history. These women called traitors, what was their treachery? Neither Pocahontas nor Nanye'hi handed over lands or people to the whiteman. For one thing, it would not have been in the Native consciousness to do so. Land was given by Creator. Neither woman gave up secrets or culture. These women knew what was in their vision. These woman lived with spirits.

In 1757, Nanye'hi married a white trader, Bryant Ward. She had a daughter, Elizabeth. Bryant Ward did not live with Nanye'hi and the Cherokee. Why? My own guess is that Nanye'hi didn't want him to. She sent him away after her child was born. The words of Pocahontas come back to me — "It is enough the child liveth." Were these Nanye'hi's words also? Did she have a vision of a New People also?

In 1775, the Watauga Purchase took place. Twenty

million acres of Cherokee land were "sold" to the British for two thousand pounds. There is no record of Nanye'hi's voice, but a woman who always counselled "never sell the land," must have been frightened and appalled at what she saw as a break in Cherokee tradition and culture. But already, whether because of her arrangement with Bryant Ward, or the adoption of white values by some of her people, Nanye'hi was losing her influence.

In 1776, a Cherokee faction led by Dragging Canoe and Old Abram set siege to the Watauga fort. They captured a white woman, Lydia Bean, and were going to burn her alive. It is said that Nanye'hi stepped to the fire and shouted, "No woman shall be burned at the stake while I am still Beloved Woman." This story has a familiar ring to it, but it is true. Cherokee men, after years of staving off the whiteman, were nevertheless learning from him. The very notion of murdering a woman, regardless of her being non-Cherokee, reflects how Native beliefs were being swept away by colonialism. In all the horror stories that have been told since we first laid eyes on the whiteman, I find this one the most telling — how Native attitudes towards women changed and became more and more like the oppressors'. This change was not every-where, and not in everyone, but enough change to freeze the blood and enrage the heart. Nanye'hi must have felt similar horror. For if attitudes towards women could go against Creator's wishes, what other terrors would follow? This is not to say that we Native peoples brought this destruction upon ourselves. Such a statement would be untrue. But this change in a religious worldview surely helped to lay us open to the self-doubt and self-loathing imposed by the "Manifest Destiny" that tore the material of our Nations.

After saving Lydia's life, Nanye'hi took this woman to live at Chote, Nanye'hi's ancestral home. History does not tell us how long they lived together, or what they talked of together. Did they talk of politics and raising children? Did they become lovers? One thing is known — Nanye'hi learned to make butter and cheese from the milk of the "whiteman's buffalo." She later used this knowledge to introduce dairying into the Cherokee Nation. But what of Lydia Bean? Did she learn of the spirits? Did she learn that women's voices were the means to Creator? Did she become assimilated into a Native way of seeing and being? I want to know the answers to these questions because it is essential to the tenuous discussion that is taking place between Native and non-Native women. I am reminded of a time when Denise and I went to Tyendinaga for a visit. We stayed with one of my many great-aunts and cousins living there. One night we sat at the kitchen table, shelling beans. We sat for a few hours, five of us, doing women's work — making food for the family. There was a magic to that evening, probably because we were performing a simple and primal act of love. Denise, always aware she is a white woman among the Mohawk, felt loved and filled to be part of this act. We Mohawk women felt the same. I think of that evening, especially when I am asked to speak or read in unfamiliar places. Lydia and Nanye'hi made food together — physically and spiritually. Surely this is a possibility for us. Pocahontas saw a new world, filled with new people. Can we be less visionary than she?

War intensified between the Cherokee and the emerging American nation. The Cherokee found themselves defeated at every turn, while Nanye'hi stood her ground and shouted for peace. In 1781, trying to negotiate a peace treaty, she cried, "Peace...let it continue. This peace must last forever. Let your children be ours. Our children will be yours. Let your women hear our words." The idea that differing races could belong to each other in family and love is the most radical of ideas. Did the white women hear Nanye'hi's words? It is doubtful. How could they have heard unless their men chose to tell them?

The year 1785 found Nanye'hi living at Chote with her children and grandchildren. Elizabeth had married an Indian agent. Her two children by Kingfisher had married and produced children. She had also opened her home to orphans, of which there were many. Deep changes were occurring within the Cherokee Nation. In 1817, the last Cherokee Council meeting was held, and Nanye'hi was expected to speak and bring counsel. Old and ill, she sent her son Fivekiller to represent her and to read her written message. And here I have another question. Nanye'hi was a literate woman, *where are her words?* As a Native woman it makes me weep to know that "history" has not deemed it worthwhile to note that Nanye'hi and Pocahontas could write and think and feel, and therefore must have put ideas and thought onto paper. Nanye'hi and Lydia must have corresponded. Where are these precious documents I long to see? Were they lost? Were they thrown away like *we* have been thrown away? Were they burned — like the truth of their lives was burned out of history and memory? Fivekiller read his mother's message to the people, words that have survived history:

Your mothers, your sisters, ask you not to part with any more of our land. We say you are our descendants and must listen to our request. Keep the land for our growing children for it was the good will of Creator to place us here.

Keep your hands off of paper for it is our own country.
If it was not, they (the whiteman) would not ask you to
put your hands on paper. It would be impossible to remove
us all for as soon as one child is raised, we have others
in our arms. Therefore children, don't part with any more
of our land but continue on it and enlarge your farms
and cultivate and raise corn so we may never go hungry.
Listen to the talks of your sisters. I have a great many
grandchildren and I wish them to do well on the land.

Nanye'hi's words were a prophecy, especially about
the impossibility of removing all the people from the land.
Even during the forced removal of southeastern Nations
to Oklahoma, known as the Trail of Tears, many Cherokee
escaped and blended into other families and races.
Nanye'hi died in 1818. She had lived a long life as
compared to Pocahontas. When she died, there were no
last words reported, but her great-grandson said that a
light rose from her body and fluttered like a bird around
her body and her family in attendance; then flew in the
direction of ancestral land. If Nanye'hi had spoken last
words, I imagine they would have been Cherokee words
she had spoken all her life — Don't sell our land. Let the
women hear my words. Our cry is for peace.

My friend Awiakta, Cherokee writer and champion of
Nanye'hi, has told me of the historic reunion of the
Cherokee Eastern and Western Councils in 1984 at the
Red Clay Historical area in East Tennessee. "These are the
same council grounds," Awiakta said, "where the last
council met before the Removal and also where Nanye'hi
came during her lifetime. (Her homesite and grave are in
the vicinity.) The Cherokee had carried the Sacred Fire
with them on the Trail of Tears. At the Reunion they
brought brands of it back. On a hill, in a receptacle made

of native stone, they relit the Sacred Fire which will burn eternally." Awiakta also said that 20,000 people were there, the descendants of Nanye'hi's vision of a new world. Red and white, Red and Black, Red, white and Black. All these glorious mixtures come together as family. "Let your children be ours. Our children will be yours." How prophetic those words!

What is history? Does it still lie in the domain of the whiteman who churns it out according to *his* politic? What is women's history? Is it still the history of white women who were privileged by their birth? Will history become something new — a story of all Nations — instead of the story of European conquest? I am a grandmother and I feel it is imperative that I tell the truthful story of the Americas. My grandsons will need this story to help them grow into good men — the kind of men our Nations deserve. My grandsons — so many kinds of blood flow in their veins. Among the four of them flows the blood of Mohawk, Irish, Scots, Polish, Cree, French, Norwegian, Cherokee — the blood of the future.

Writing Life

I'm wondering if it might be a good time to make bread. The writing is not going well. Truthfully, it's not going. Perhaps the soothing action of mixing and kneading would get me back to a good place. The writing. the writing. It takes on large proportions in my mind. It is not easy to write. Nor is it fun, and pleasant is not a word I would use in conjunction with writing. Yet, it is hard to relax when I'm away from the computer and my desk. I keep thinking about the stories. I dream at night about the people in the stories. I see their faces in odd places — in the grocery store, on the street, sitting on a subway, lurking behind a tree or bush. They are like ghosts. But ghosts have had a life. These people are looking to me to help give them life.

In the kitchen I assemble the yeast, the flour, sugar, oil and take down the large stainless steel bowl. Turning on the tap, I empty two packets of yeast into the bowl. Running my wrist under the water to test the temperature, I judge it to be right. I measure two cups of water into the bowl. The yeast bubbles up, then sinks to the bottom.

This is a metaphor.

I stir the yeast and water with a wooden spoon and think about my dad. Daddy. I think of him often, missing him, wondering what he is doing in the Spirit World.

I add sugar, dry milk, and a little oil to the yeast-water.

I stir, adding flour by the handful until the dough is a good consistency. I dump the mixture onto the cutting board and add still more flour to the spongy mass. I begin to knead — pushing it away with the heels of my hands, pulling it towards me — I make a rhythm.

When my dad was young, he discovered music — a certain kind of music. He was walking in a neighbourhood in Oshawa, Ontario, and heard music coming out of a window. He'd never heard music like that. He wanted to walk up to the house, ring the doorbell and ask what that music was. But he was a little Native boy, and little Native boys didn't ring doorbells and ask questions on a street that was white. He never said what he was doing on that particular street and I never asked — the story was enough.

The story is always enough for me, but editors insist on explanations, details. Does it matter how he got from here to there? Does it matter? Isn't story why we are here, no matter the mode of transportation? Daddy said that when he grew up and was earning some money, he found out the name of the music he had heard on that Oshawa street — Beethoven's Ninth Symphony. He bought the recording, then a year later bought a record player, played it over and over, and sang "Ode to Joy" ever after. I like that story. It testifies to a number of things that Daddy taught me — beauty is possible, and beauty is found in unlikely places. All his stories were about that, all of my stories are about that.

I knead the dough and hum "Ode to Joy." I never planned on being a writer. It was not even a fantasy of mine. Born in an urban Mohawk family, story was a given, not something to search for or discover. But the gift of *writing* came a long time after my birth. Forty years after.

That year I was on a search for the spirit of Molly Brant, Clan Mother, elder sister of Chief Joseph Brant and the architect of diplomatic relations between the Mohawk Nation and the British. My lover, Denise, and I were, at that time, caterers and bakers. We worked in our home (illegally) making desserts, quiche, breads, and various other items for small, local restaurants. We also were called upon to cater political events — conferences, seminars, benefits, readings, visual artists' openings. We did not make a lot of money, but enough to pay the bills and take care of our family, consisting of us and my three daughters. We had planned a camping trip in the East, stopping at Tyendinaga, my Reserve, then moving on to New York state. I wanted to visit all the homes in which Molly Brant had resided, just to see where she had walked, where she had slept, where she had dreamed. Her story has always been neglected in favour of her brother's, Joseph; just one more example of sexist racism at work. I didn't know what I was going to do with this knowledge or the feelings I would uncover, but I just wanted to *see* her with my own heart. Grandma Brant always told us that Molly was the true warrior and truth-carrier of the Brant history. We proceeded on our trip, stopping at Brantford, on to Six Nations to Tyendinaga (where Molly Brant never lived, but where my family did and does), on to New York state and the towns where Sir William Johnson and his "country wife" had made homes.

I wash out the bowl, oil it, and place the mound of kneaded dough inside, covering everything with a tea-towel. That trip changed my life, changed what image I had of myself; intensified my love of all things Native, all those things that make culture alive and real. It was while we were coming back to Michigan that we decided to take another road through what used to be Seneca land. The dirt road looped through stands of White Pine and deciduous growth. We were coming around a curve in the road, Denise driving, when a great shadow blocked out the sunlight and the tip of a wing touched the front windshield. A Bald Eagle made his presence known to us. Denise stopped the car, I opened the door and stood, transfixed, as Eagle made a circle around us then flew to a nearby White Pine and settled himself on a branch. The branch dipped low from his weight, his dark wings folded around him, his white head touched by a flash of sunlight through the needles of the tree. I remember how his great talons gripped the branch as I moved closer and stood in front of him, my heart drumming inside my human body. We were locked together in vision. I could feel his heartbeat take over mine. I felt my hands curving and holding onto the branch. I felt the sunlight flashing on my head. I heard the thoughts; the deep, scratching thoughts of blood, bone and prey, the thoughts of wind carrying me along, the thoughts of heartbeat. He blinked his eyes, unfolded his wings, and flew away. I watched him as I slowly came back to myself, to the smell around me, the breeze picking up and scattering dust in my face, my legs growing so weak I could hardly walk back to the car. When I got home, I began to write.

I was born in 1941, in the house of my Grandma and Grandpa Brant — the house where my Aunt Colleen still lives. It was a hot May morning, as my Irish-Scots mother pushed and willed me out of her womb. The story goes that Daddy had bought an ice-cream-on-a-stick for my mom, but in the excitement, put it in his pocket. It wasn't until Grandma was doing the wash that she discovered the mess and made Daddy wash his own pants. I grew up in a family that had strong women and sweet men. Mama's family was not thrilled to have her marry an Indian, in fact her father refused to give her away at the wedding and railed and stormed about having a "nigger" for a son-in-law. In time he came around, but those kinds of wounds were not easy to close or heal.

I have a photograph of my mom and dad around the time they were newly married. They were ages eighteen and twenty. The old black and white photograph shows my mom wearing shorts and a halter top, Daddy dressed in a short-sleeved shirt and pants. They are leaning against a honeysuckle vine, Daddy's arms around Mama's bare waist. She is leaning against his chest, head thrown back with laughter. She is holding his hands that encircle her waist. They look so young, so sensual, so in love, so happy to be touching and smelling the honeysuckle that twists around Daddy's dark hair and comes to rest on Mama's blonde head. I came from this — this union of white and Native.

Mama and Daddy came to live with the Brant family. In the old way, the traditional way, Daddy would have gone to live with the Smiths. But since Mama was a white woman and feelings were bad on their side, it was the natural course of things that the Brants would assimilate her and all offspring of the union. Thus, I was born in the Little Room of Grandma and Grandpa's house in Detroit, the room that was alternately used as a birthing room, a sick room, a room to put up various members of the family when they came to visit or to live.

Memories are stories — pictures of the mind, gathered up and words put to them, making them live and breathe. My memories are good ones. I was loved.

There were a lot of us, living in that small house. Grandma, Grandpa, Auntie, Mom and Dad, and their three children. At other times there were more — aunts, uncles and their children, relatives from Tyendinaga with their families. I wonder to this day how we all fit, how we managed to all sit around the kitchen table. (The young kids usually ate in the Little Room off a card table. It was a rite of passage when we became old enough to sit with the grown-ups. Like most of what Grandma did, she had her own way of deciding who was old enough. I think I sat with the adults when I turned twelve, but others got there before their twelfth year, and some had to wait much longer.) When my cousins and I get together, we inevitably get around to talking about that card table and the question of space. How did we all fit? Was there some magic involved?

There were books. Both Grandma and Grandpa knew how to read and write. They considered it a blessing. They read a lot and always bought the newspaper. Grandma was a Methodist and read a verse from the Bible every night before she went to bed. And she insisted on saying grace before meals. "Our heavenly father, we ask you to bless this food for the use of our souls and bodies. In Jesus' name we ask it. Amen." Grandpa was not a christian, preferring the old way, the Mohawk way. Yet, for all of Grandma's high-mindedness about christianity, she believed most fervently in the power and beauty of Earth. Her garden was a testament to that belief.

The first inklings of connection and intimacy with Land came from watching and helping Grandma and Grandpa work the garden. Getting the soil ready, using the planting stick, seeds drifting from their hands, I felt the devotion and care they lavished on that small piece of land. When we would take trips to Tyendinaga (our Territory and the place they were born and raised) I felt that connection even more deeply. This is where they came from. This is where Daddy came from. This is where I came from. This is where our people's bones are buried and revered. This is *home*.

Grandpa taught me Mohawk and the idea of what men are supposed to be — loving, hard workers, giving, secure, respectful of women, playful with children. Grandma taught me manners, how to make corn soup and fry bread, and the idea of what women are supposed to be — strong, fierce protectors of family and land, independent of men while respecting them. (If they warranted respect. She held no affection for men who drank, neglected family, or hurt children and women.) Grandma never needed a man to tell her how to fix a toilet, clean a well, or butcher a deer. And her daughters, my aunts, followed her counsel. Even my mother became like that. She must have gathered the knowledge by osmosis. Those two grandparents formed many of my values and the beliefs I hold to.

I get up to check the bread. It has a smooth, glossy look to it. I poke my finger in gently and the bread rises up to cover the hole. I punch it down, cut it in two pieces, make two loaves and place them in the bread pans.

When I began to write, I wrote about my family. At first there were funny stories about my grandparents' Indian ways. Nice stories, full of loving description of their ways with each other and with the world outside them. Then something happened. The writing got more serious; my family was not just fun — they were also survivors of colonial oppression. I began to figure out, through the writing, that what I remembered was not necessarily the complete truth. I was still viewing the family through the eyes of the child I had been.

What happens when I sit in front of the computer (or, in those days, the typewriter)? This desire to peel back the husk of memory, the hungry need to find the food that is waiting inside. There are times when I feel as if *I* am the seed, being watered and sunned by the keys I press to make words. The words are the shoot, wandering across the screen, stopping then starting, coming from my mouth, my fingers. I speak aloud as I write — the words being borne from mouth to hand. Somewhere in that activity is the nucleus of writing, of truth. I no longer feel that the words come directly from me. There are spirits at work who move my lips, my fingers. Who call me, who take over my clumsy attempts to put one word after the other to make some kind of sense. An automatic writing of sorts. I used to fight the spirits. Now I accept them.

I check the loaves. They have risen nicely. I place them in the oven at 375 degrees, close the door and think about the work that is piled on my desk. There are deadlines for articles, correspondence to write, a book to finish, another book making itself known at the edges of my mind. I procrastinate. I avoid the inevitable confrontation with the spirits of writing. I have been known to clean the whole house to the extent of cleaning cupboards, just to keep from doing what the screen asks me to reveal. Why? At this point in my life, I have written about most things that others might shy away from — my life with an abusive, alcoholic husband, my life with Denise, my lesbianism, sexual lovers — yet, there is always the modesty, and the fear of being judged and therefore, all Mohawks being judged. The writing spirit has no fear, has no human failings that waste time procrastinating. There are times when I think the spirit is the collected consciousness of those Native writers who have passed on — Pauline Johnson, D'Arcy McNickle; they can't stop writing, even in the Spirit World, and have to make visitations to those of us on Earth who call ourselves writers. And while I have accepted their presence in my life, I still want to ask — why me? They do not answer.

There was a time when I was ashamed to be Indian. This happened around the time I was in the fifth or sixth grade. I was a pale, blonde child, I wore glasses, and had lots of baby fat. Until then, I was ashamed of my lightness, my paleness. The family was dark — dark skin, dark hair, dark eyes — and then there was me. I used to wonder if I was the right child, or if I was somehow switched at birth. Since I was born at home and there were no other babies around, this fantasy didn't last long. I was very jealous of my cousins who "looked" Mohawk. They had the dark hair I envied, the brown or dark grey eyes I wanted to peer out of my own face. I resented my mother — somehow this was her fault. But as I grew older and caught the drift of racism, I hid my Mohawk self from the schoolmates who might have become my tormentors, had they known. It was enough that I was fat and wore glasses; taunting and teasing waited for me if I made myself noticed. At home, life went on pretty much as usual. The family was not aware of my "other life" as a white girl. My girlfriends in the neighbourhood didn't give a whole lot of thought to the family. Anyway, they had grown up on the street that had the only Indian family. This was nothing new or different to them. But the other kids in school were to be feared, cajoled, envied.

My writing soon took an autobiographical bent. I got

published fairly soon, a fact that causes me amazement even today. My work in those days was raw, not as free from cliche or roughness, but editors saw something. There was a substantial network of feminist journals and magazines in the early 80s. They took chances on women like me — women who had no prior publishing experience, women who were not "educated," women of colour. Taking chances was the hallmark of these publications, and I am very thankful for their existence.

It seemed that Eagle had many plans for me. In 1982, I was asked to edit a special issue of *Sinister Wisdom*, a feminist journal at that time published and edited by Adrienne Rich and Michelle Cliff. I took on the job, not because I knew anything about editing, but because the issue was to be about Native women. This caused me a lot of excitement *and* fear. In the first place, until that time, there had not been an anthology of exclusively Native women's work. All other Native anthologies had been edited by whites. *A Gathering of Spirit* was a ground-breaker in those two areas, but also in another equally important area. Of the sixty women who had contributed to the book, ten of us declared our lesbianism. This was a new day in the history of Aboriginal writing. This time around, we were actively saying who we were — all parts of us — no coyness, or hiding, or pretending to be something we weren't. It was a great political and personally courageous act on the part of those nine women who stood with me. I will always be thankful to them and blessed in knowing them.

Another wonderful thing about *A Gathering of Spirit*, is the humanness of the book. This is not just another anthology of well-known and well-published authors. There are first-time writers, voices from Native women in prison, letters, oral histories, artwork. This was a special book in 1983. It continues to be a special book today. Native women write to tell me how the book changed their lives. Many of the women who were published for the first time, now have their own books. And many Two-Spirits thank me for shaking the stereotype of what makes good writing, what makes good Native writing — it is not all male, or heterosexual, or necessarily from the pen of someone who had formal western education. I am very proud of that book. Not because I edited it, but because it changed the face of Native literature forever. It became its own entity. It became what it had to be — a brilliant and loving weapon of change.

I published my first book of poems and stories, *Mohawk Trail*, in 1985. Although I like this book and continue to read some of the work in public performance, I am always chagrined when people mention a piece from it. I want to say, "That old stuff," not because I don't like the work, but because each *new* work seems better to me, more full and mature. Perhaps this is the way with writers. My book of short stories, *Food & Spirits*, was published in 1991. There was a long gap between books because I am not a prolific writer; I don't write every day, yet I write in my head every day. I listen to people's conversations, not because I'm a voyeur, but because I am fascinated with people's voices — the rhythm, the phrases they use, the accents, the music. I keep these some place inside me; even in sleep, words from a conversation flash by; people's faces pop up, some I've never seen before. Linda Hogan once said that she used to think she was crazy, but then she realized that the craziness was due to being a half-breed in a white world. I believe that too. I also believe that being a Native writer induces its own madness. We are trying to make sense out of the senseless. We are trying to tell a truth in a culture that dishonours truth-tellers and the story behind the telling.

Grandpa died when I was quite young. I remember the wake, his body laid out in the wooden box, the family and strangers all over the place. I hated it. It scared me. I wasn't quite sure that he was really dead, or if he would rise up (like one of the stories in Grandma's bible). If Grandpa was really dead, who would talk with me in Mohawk? (By one of those generational twists, a result of colonialism, my father and his siblings didn't speak the language, but understood it. I suspect that Grandma had a lot to do with this. Although she remained adamantly and vehemently Mohawk, she also felt that it was okay to assimilate "a little," for safety's sake.) If Grandpa was really dead, how would we all survive? We depended on him for so much, not just economically, but emotionally and spiritually. Who would counteract Grandma's forays into christian platitudes? Who would hug me tight and call me his "masterpiece?" Who would make the raspberry jam every year, the bright red jars decorating the fruit cellar?

Grandma died when I was eighteen, newly married and a mother. My husband had been in the Navy and we were living in a forsaken town in Georgia. There was no money for me to come home, so the family decided they wouldn't tell me about the death until after the wake. I was furious. I felt that I was given no choice. It's true there was no money, but I would have liked to have said goodbye to Grandma at her moment of death, not after she was in the ground. It was years before I found myself at the cemetery where they both were buried. It had taken me that long to be able to see that place, that land of death. And many years after that, I took my two oldest grandsons, Nathanael and Benjamin to visit. They rolled on the markers, picked up leaves and threw them at each other, shouted and laughed. I wondered how often a cemetery gets to hear the laughter of children. I tell my grandsons about their great-great-grandparents. My memory will shift to theirs, and they will keep the stories alive and moving.

My marriage was not a good one. I was seventeen and pregnant. My dad didn't want me to marry. My mom did. She often would have these attacks of caring what people thought of her. I suppose her great rebellion in marrying my dad took its toll on her in little ways. She would compensate by drilling us in proper behaviour and morals. I don't know what I wanted. I guess I wanted to be grown-up and living a grown-up life. I thought that marriage guaranteed that. Also, my mom and dad genuinely loved and liked each other. I had no idea that my marriage wouldn't be the same. But, in the first place, my husband wasn't a sweet Mohawk man. We were to live out the fourteen years together in anger, violence, alcohol, hatred. But I had three daughters, Kimberly, Jennifer, Jill; and they were in turn the only sweetness and beauty that was visible to me during those fourteen years.

Leave him I did; or rather, told him to leave us. I went on welfare, looked for work, tried to hold it together. My parents were wonderful — buying food, buying the kids' clothes, taking care of things when I felt I couldn't. They had always been there during the course of my marriage, but I couldn't bring myself to tell them just how many times he came home drunk, the marital rape, the screaming and shouting. I was ashamed to tell them, as if *I* had brought this to be. Daddy, slow to anger, would have erupted and probably done harm to my husband and brought harm to himself. My mother would have wanted to find a way to take care of it that would reduce me to a child again. I kept all of it secret, only daring, years later, to expose the secrets through writing.

I do not believe that all writing is autobiographical, or that a writer has to use words as a confessional. In fact, I think that type of writing is unique to white North America. I do know that as a Mohawk woman, I was born to and grew up in a culture that persists and resists, but also carries its load of colonialist untruths. As an Aboriginal woman, I have internalized these untruths. Writing helps me to let go. The spirits of writing bring comfort, assurance, righteous anger, deliverance. I am alive, quivering, in front of the computer. I dredge but also bury. I face the monsters of racism, homophobia, woman-hating, with the spirits beside me. I am protected at the same time as I open myself to rage. I find salvation while uncovering horror. Writing is the place to feel all senses commingle and cohabit, bringing forth something new, giving birth to words, to beings that will inhabit story, that *are* story. This is what the spirits bring — verdant sensuality, lush panoply, a garden.

I check the bread. It is rising, developing a golden crust. It is almost done, almost there.

I met Denise Dorsz in 1976. I immediately loved her. For me, it was simple — I wanted to make a life with this woman. I wanted to share my life with her. Denise has brought many gifts to my life; we have also had to struggle and fight for the ability of each of us to be separate and unique while building a partnership of love and continuity. Denise is white — Polish-American — and is also twelve years younger than me. The romanticising of the lesbian and gay community is hard to dispel. We often believe the myth that is not exclusive to heterosexuals — fall in love, live happily ever after. As of this writing, in 1994, we have been together for eighteen years. There was a period of time when we were separated, and I wrote exhaustively and excessively during that time about our relationship, about our separation. None of this was for publication, but then, none of what I write is consciously or unconsciously for anyone else but me and the spirits. My point is that I was able to use writing to heal a wound that was very deep and festering. I was angry — writing brought me calm. I was obsessing about the past — writing gave me insight into the future. I was in pain — writing cooled the pain, brought me out of that condition. Writing was/is Medicine. It is the only thing I know that brings complete wholeness while it is making a visitation. Making love comes close — orgasm, like writing, is a spiritual communication.

I never went to university. My circumstances were such that it was unthinkable to even imagine going. Yet, my father had worked days in the auto factory and gone to college at night. Formal education was not unheard of or dismissed in the family. My grandparents thought highly of it, Daddy and Mama worked tirelessly to achieve it for my father. My siblings and I were encouraged, prodded to achieve a degree of some kind, and my sister and brother worked extremely hard to get those degrees. Instead, I married and gave up all desires for expansion of myself. It was 1959; this is what women did, especially self-hating ones like me. Why did I hate myself? There is no simple political polemic that can explain or describe my actions. I was loved by my family. I had solid and sturdy role models. I had culture. I had language. I had a spiritual base. Then again, I inherited secrets. They wore me down. I learned to be silent, rather than reveal the family I wanted to idealize.

The secrets of Indigenous life are not secret. Alcoholism, family violence, the internalized violence of self-doubt, self-loathing. My father, who was a brilliant man, used to say in serio-comic fashion, "What do I know, I'm just a dumb Indian." He knew he wasn't, yet *did not know* if he was just that. I have also made that statement, but more than that, I have thought it and felt it. Writing has changed my perception of myself. Eagle has changed my way of being in this life.

Writing. This mysterious and magical act that brings possibility of transformation. I do not believe that what I have to say is more important than others' words. At the same time, there is a reason why I am able to bead words together to make language. It makes me able to be of use: to my people, to the many families I am connected to — First Nations, feminist, gay and lesbian, working-class, human. I love words. When I was in the sixth grade, I won a spelling-bee and my prize was a dictionary. I loved that book — so many words to choose from, so many words to play with. To this day, I write with a dictionary beside me, sometimes forgetting what I'm writing as I turn the pages of that book, reading the meanings, the way words came into being. Yet, there are times when English words are not full enough or circular enough to encompass a thought or feeling I am trying to convey. It is then that I mourn for the loss of my Mohawk language. With no one to speak it with after Grandpa died, I have forgotten the words, but not the wholeness and richness of the meaning behind the words. I believe

120

my language is hovering somewhere inside the place where the writing spirits dwell. They will bring it back to me. And there are times when Mohawk words jump into the computer, a surprise, a lovely gift when I least expected them to come.

I loved to read. I began reading at age four, taught by Grandpa and my dad. I remember the book, *Johnny Had a Nickel*, a book about a kid who had a nickel to spend and the long list of things he could buy with it (this was 1945, don't forget). Johnny ended up going for a ride on a carousel, but I ended up with an obsession for words, and a great respect for books. I had a library card when I was five. The library was fascinating to me — still is. I thought people who wrote books were creatures different from us. I didn't know until I was well into adulthood that Native people wrote books, and that Pauline Johnson, a Mohawk writer, had been published in the last century. My family didn't know either, or we would have had those books in our home. I read everything and anything I could get my hands on. It's cliché, but books were my friends. Along with movies, they shaped my view of the society I lived in. I always knew that my family was not a part of that society, didn't *want* to be a part of that society. Ah, but how *I* wanted to be (at least during my childhood and teen-age years). I wanted to be an actress like Ava Gardner, Rita Hayworth; I wanted to dance like Marge Champion, sing like Ella Fitzgerald or June Christy (I seemed to have a lot of confusion about where my loyalties lay — with the white girls or the women of colour! Maybe this is what being a half-breed means). I wanted to be acceptable. It wasn't until I was grown that I picked up a book by James Baldwin, and found the kind of words and world that had meaning for me, personally. Though he wrote from the culture of African-Americans, he wrote about the effects of racism, the effects of colonialism, and I found the missing words that had left me bereft of meaning in my life. Later on, I was to "discover" Scott Momaday, James Welch, Simon Ortiz, Paula Gunn Allen — people of my own kind, people who wrote about *us*.

The timer is ringing. The bread-smells are permeating the house. I open the oven, the heat fogging my glasses. For a moment, I can't see, caught in another way of being. I lift my head, hearing the faint whispers of spirits gathering together. My glasses clear, I remove the bread from the oven, tapping it, hearing that hollow sound that signifies a good loaf of bread. I turn the loaves onto the counter and return to the computer. I turn it on — a low hum emits as I tap in the code to lay the screen bare and accepting.

In most of my work, especially the short stories, I attempt to show break-throughs in people's lives. Much of my own life has involved breaking through existing scenarios that have been programmed into my head. Despite the loving and culturally rich messages I received from the family, the cacophony of the dominant society made an even louder noise. Through writing, I "come back" to the family, come back to who I am, and *why* I am. The noise of dominance recedes and gives over to the music of my ancestors, my history. The people who inhabit my stories, inhabit my life. They have made a home inside me, inside the computer, on the page. The people who live in story are, like Native people every-where, struggling and dreaming, caught between the beauty of what we know, and the ugliness of what has been done to our people, our land. It seems as though I give these people choices — like the choice I make every day — to resist the ugly and go with the beauty. I say, "it seems," because I never know what the people are going to do; they tell me. I feel as though they are speaking, "Write me, write me," and I have to struggle against what I have been told from white society, free myself, and give myself over to the singing and whispering that is my world, the world of Indigenous being.

When I was finishing up a book of essays, my father, whose physical body died in 1991, came to sit with me. My father, who never wrote a book, but wanted to, oh how he wanted to, was with me, chastising me over sentences that wouldn't live, "Now, Bella, you know that doesn't sound right," praising me when I got it right, "That's good, Daughter, that's good." His life, which was often so circumscribed, was one of hope and faith. He believed in the continuation of the People. He believed in the old way, the *Onkwehonwe* way. He believed that the best was always to come. He left Earth with that faith gleaming in his eyes, transported to the Spirit World where he probably sings "Ode to Joy" to his relatives. It is my turn, my inheritance to sing an ode to the continuity of Mohawk ethos.

The bread is made. Later on tonight, Denise and I will cut it, slather on the butter, the same butter I am told is bad for my arteries. I'll save some for my grandsons, four examples of how story continues in the blood.

The computer is humming. The cursor blinks and talks, calling me into the sacred territory of story and meaning. They are gathering more forcefully now, the alchemy about to begin. Alchemy — from the Greek word Khemia, meaning Black Land — the Black Land of these words appearing on an electronic machine, soon to be transmuted into words on paper, the flesh of trees. What happens after, no longer has to do with me. I've done my job.

A Beginning Bibliography

Allen, Paula Gunn. *The Woman Who Owned The Shadows*. San Francisco: Spinsters/Aunt Lute, 1983.

Anzaldua, Gloria, ed. *This Bridge Called My Back*. Albany: Kitchen Table Press, 1981.

Armstrong, Jeanette. *Slash*. Penticton: Theytus, 1986.

Arnott, Joanne. *Wiles of Girlhood*. Vancouver: Press Gang, 1991.

------. *My Grass Cradle*. Vancouver: Press Gang, 1993.

Awiakta. *Selu: Seeking the Corn Mother*. Golden: Fulcrum, 1993.

Baskin, Cyndy. *The Invitation*. Toronto: Sister Vision, 1993.

Baker, Marie. *Being on the Moon*. Vancouver: Polestar, 1990.

Bell, Betty Louise. *Faces In the Moon*. Norman: University of Oklahoma Press, 1994.

Brant, Beth, ed. *A Gathering of Spirit*. California: Sinister Wisdom Books, 1984; Ithaca: Firebrand, 1988; Toronto: Women's Press, 1989.

------. *Mohawk Trail* Ithaca: Firebrand: 1985; Toronto: Women's Press, 1990.

------. *Food & Spirits*. Ithaca: Firebrand and Vancouver: Press Gang, 1991.

Broker, Ignatia. *Night Flying Woman: An Ojibway Narrative*. St. Paul: Minnesota Historical Society, 1983.

Campbell, Maria. *Halfbreed*. Toronto: McClelland & Stewart, 1973.

Chrystos. *Dream On*. Vancouver: Press Gang, 1991.

------. *Not Vanishing*. Vancouver: Press Gang, 1988.

------. *In Her I Am*. Vancouver: Press Gang, 1993.

Culleton, Beatrice. *In Search of April Raintree*. Winnipeg: Pemmican, 1983.

Cuthand, Beth. *Voices in the Waterfall*. Vancouver: Lazara, 1989.

Dauenhauer, Nora Marks. *The Droning Shaman*. Haines: The Black Currant, 1985.

Day, Sharon. *Shield*. Unpublished manuscript.

Deloria, Ella. *Water Lily*. Lincoln: University of Nebraska, 1988.

Drinnon, Richard. *Facing West: The Metaphysics of Indian Hating and*

Empire Building. Minneapolis, MN: University of Minnesota Press, 1980.

Erdrich, Louise. *The Beet Queen*. Boston: Bantam, 1989.

------. *Love Medicine*. Toronto, New York: Bantam, 1987.

------. *Tracks*. New York: Henry Holt, 1988.

Fife, Connie. *Beneath the Naked Sun*. Toronto: Sister Vision, 1992.

Fife, Connie, ed. *The Colour of Resistance*. Toronto: Sister Vision Press, 1993.

Francisco, Nia. *Blue Horses for Navajo Women*. Greenfield Center: Greenfield Review, 1988.

Freeman, Minnie. *Life Among the Qallunaat*. Edmonton: Hurtig, 1978.

French, Alice. *My Name is Masah*. Winnipeg: Penquis, 1976.

------. *Restless Nomad*. Winnipeg: Pemmican, 1991.

Glancy, Diane. *Lone Dog's Winter Count*. Albequerque: West End, 1991.

Goodleaf, Donna. Unpublished manuscript.

Gould, Janice. *Beneath My Heart*. Ithaca: Firebrand, 1990.

Hale, Janet Campbell. *Bloodlines*. New York: Harper Perennial, 1993.

Harjo, Joy. *In Mad Love and War*. Middletown: Wesleyan, 1990.

Hogan, Linda. *Mean Spirit*. New York: Atheneum; Toronto: Collier McMillan, 1990.

Hum-Ishu-Ma (Mourning Dove). *Cogewea, The Half-Blood*. Lincoln: University of Nebraska, 1981.

Joe, Rita. *Poems of Rita Joe*. Halifax: Abenaki, 1978.

Johnson, E. Pauline. *Flint & Feather*. Toronto: Hodder & Stoughton, 1931.

------. *The Moccasin Maker*. Tucson: University of Arizona, 1987.

Johnston, Verna Patronella. *I Am Nokomis, Too*. Don Mills: General Publishing Ltd., 1977.

Keller, Betty. *Pauline: A Biography of Pauline Johnson*. Vancouver: Douglas & McIntyre, 1981.

Keeshig-Tobias, Lenore. *Bird-Talk*. Toronto: Sister Vision, 1992.

Mankiller, Wilma. *Mankiller: A Chief and Her People*. New York: St. Martin's Press, 1993.

Maracle, Lee. *Bobbie Lee: Indian Rebel*. 1976; reprint, Toronto: Women's Press, 1990.

------. *Ravensong*. Vancouver: Press Gang, 1993.

Mojica, Monique. *Princess Pocahontas and The Blue Spots*. Toronto: Women's Press, 1991.

Momaday, N. Scott. *House Made of Dawn*. New York: New American Library, 1966.

Moran, Mary. *Métisse Patchwork*. Unpublished manuscript.

Nunez, Bonita Wa Wa Calachaw. *Spirit Woman*. New York: Harper & Row, 1980.

Ortiz, Simon. *From Sand Creek*. Oak Park: Thunder's Mouth, 1981.

Patterson, Ida. *Montana Memories*. Pablo: Salish Kootenai Community College, 1981.

Roscoe, Will, ed. *Living The Spirit: A Gay American Indian Anthology*. New York: St. Martin's, 1988.

Rose, Wendy. *The Halfbreed Chronicles*. Los Angeles: West End, 1985.

------. *The Zuni Man-Woman*. Albuquerque: University of New Mexico Press, 1991.

Sam-Cromarty, Margaret. *James Bay Memories*. Lakefield: Wanpoone, 1992.

Sears, Vicki. *Simple Songs*. Ithaca: Firebrand, 1990.

Silko, Leslie Marmon. *Almanac of The Dead*. New York, Toronto: Simon & Schuster, 1991.

------. *Ceremony*. New York: Viking Press, 1977.

Silvera, Makeda, ed. *Piece of My Heart*. Toronto: Sister Vision, 1991.

Slipperjack, Ruby. *Honour The Sun*. Winnipeg; Pemmican, 1987.

------. *Silent Words*. Saskatoon: Fifth House, 1992.

TallMountain, Mary. *The Light on the Tent Wall: A Bridging*. Los Angeles: University of California at Los Angeles, 1990.

Theriault, Madeline Katt. *Moose to Moccasins*. Toronto: Natural Heritage/Natural History Inc., 1992.

Tremblay, Gail. *Indian Singing in 20th Century America*. Corvallis: Calyx, 1990.

Wallis, Velma. *Two Old Women*. New York: Harper Perennial, 1993.

Walters, Anna Lee. *Ghost-Singer*. Flagstaff: Northland, 1988.

------. *Talking Indian: Reflections on Survival and Writing*. Ithaca: Firebrand, 1992.

Welch, James. *Winter in the Blood*. New York: Penguin, 1974.

Williams, Walter. *The Spirit in the Flesh*. Boston: Beacon Press, 1986.

Wolf, Helen Pease. *Reaching Both Ways*. Laramie: Jelm Mountain Publications, 1989.

Woody, Elizabeth. *Hand Into Stone*. Bowling Green: Contact II, 1988.

Zitkala-Sa. *American Indian Stories*. Washington: Hayworth, 1921.

BETH BRANT is a Bay of Quinte Mohawk from Tyendinaga Mohawk Territory in Ontario. She was born on May 6, 1941. She is the editor of *A Gathering of Spirit*, the ground-breaking collection of writing and art by Native women (Firebrand Books, USA and Women's Press, Canada). She is the author of *Mohawk Trail*, prose and poetry (Firebrand Books and Women's Press, 1985) and *Food & Spirits*, short fiction (Firebrand Books and Press Gang, 1991). Her work has appeared in numerous Native, feminist and lesbian anthologies and she has done readings, lectures and taught throughout North America. She has received an Ontario Arts Council award, a Canada Council grant and is a recipient of a National Endowment for the Arts Literature Fellowship. Beth Brant is currently working on two books, *Testimony from the Faithful*, essays about land and spirit, and *I'll Sing Til the Day I Die*, oral histories of Tyendinega Elders. She divides her time between living in Michigan and in Canada. She is a mother and grandmother and lives with her partner of eighteen years, Denise Dorsz. She has been writing since the age of forty and considers it a gift for her community.